A WHAT DOCTORS DON

CW00326530

YOUR HEALTHY

Heart

Every illness and every patient are unique. This book is intended as a source of information only. Readers are urged to work in partnership with a qualified, experienced practitioner before undertaking (or refraining from) any treatments listed in these pages.

ISBN 0 953473 1 4

For all our readers

ABOUT WHAT DOCTORS DON'T TELL YOU

What Doctors Don't Tell You, the publisher of Your Healthy Heart, has been telling people about the secrets of orthodox medicine for nearly 10 years. Its principle publication is the monthly newsletter of the same name, which was first published in 1989. Today, it is read by subscribers in over 100 countries around the world, who have come to rely on its in-depth research. The company has also published 24 booklets on specific health issues.

Its sister publication is PROOF!, a quarterly newsletter that looks at the scientific evidence for alternative treatments and remedies. The company also publishes a magazine, Natural Parent, which promotes alternative and holistic ideas about parenting.

To find out more about What Doctors Don't Tell You and its sister publications, please write to: WDDTY, 77 Grosvenor Avenue, London N5 2NN, tel: 0171 354 4592, fax: 0171 354 8907, or e-mail: wddty@zoo.co.uk.

What Doctors Don't Tell You editor is Lynne McTaggart, an award-winning journalist and author, who regularly appears on TV and radio, as well as in the national press.

CONTENTS

Introduction

INTRODUCTION

The number of deaths from heart disease reads like a terrifying roll-call of modern times. Although cancer, stroke and even iatrogenic illness are close runners-up, heart disease is still firmly out front as the number one killer in the West. A decade ago, one million people died of heart disease in the US, and a further 160,000 in the UK. Although we hear about tremendous strides made in the treatment of heart patients and sophisticated breakthroughs in prevention, today's statistics since that time tell a very different story.

In the US, despite the fact that the benefits of the low-fat diet have permeated the national consciousness, despite the development of a food, pharmaceutical and medical monolith devoted entirely to heart-disease prevention, despite the ready availability of the latest in gee-whizz drugs and surgery and renewed faith in aspirin as a way to avoid vascular incidents, heart disease continues to kill more Americans than anything else. Heart disease in the US has dramatically risen between 1940 and 1996—from 86.7 per 100,000 to 187.1 per 100,000. These figures, prepared for the American Heart Association's 1999 Heart and Stroke Statistical Update (BMJ, 1999; 318: 79), translate into 400,000 Americans developing congestive heart failure each year. In all, one-fifth—or 58.8 million—of Americans still suffer from cardiovascular disease, and more than half of all Americans have above average total cholesterol concentrations.

Heart disease fell between 1979 and 1989, by 30 per cent, but researchers don't seem to have an explanation, save that perhaps people are smoking less in the States.

Although medicine has helped more people who survive the first attack to avoid the second, it has done little to stop deaths the first time around. Of the 1.5 million people who suffer a heart attack in the US each year, just 350,000 live to tell the tale. In other words, the first heart attack is often the last.

Not surprisingly, with these sort of statistics, much of medical research is devoted to understanding the causes of heart disease. Since the Sixties, when doctors first hypothesised that lowering blood cholesterol levels would prevent heart attacks and strokes, everyone in the West has fixated upon cholesterol as the primary cause of heart failure. Slightly elevated blood pressure runs a close second as a risk factor to be prevented at all cost.

Nevertheless, virtually every week, a piece of research is published offering contrary findings to a previous paper. Indeed, one study reckoned that all the most popular so-called standard risk factors—smoking, high blood pressure and cholesterol—accounted for no more than 50 per cent of the total risk (JAMA, 1993; 269: 998-1003).

More than a decade ago, What Doctors Don't Tell You was one of the first publications to blow the whistle on heart-disease prevention and treatment as largely misguided and unproven. In issue after issue, we reported on studies showing that altering risk factors like cholesterol levels doesn't do any good and indeed may do harm.

In fact, the more recent studies show that lowering cholesterol through drugs and diet actually increases your chances of dying in ways that we don't yet fully understand.

Many of the other, so-called miracle cures for heart disease also haven't stood the test of time. Angioplasty, which has been touted as a safer alternative to bypass surgery, offers benefits that seldom last. And bypass surgery, while a medical marvel, is only helpful in very specific situations.

Although medicine considers that any adversary this formidable can be licked only by the most sophisticated of medical gadgetry, many alternative treatments can work far better in treating arterial disease, heart attacks or high blood pressure. Alternative medicine, which often employs a holistic approach, also tackles a proven cause of heart disease—isolation. For all of its clever machinery, modern medicine doesn't take into account that most people with heart disease are literally dying of a broken heart.

To produce this booklet, we have pulled together the best of the evidence we've gathered over the years on alternative and conventional approaches to the most common heart problems. We've also examined many of the new non-conventional approaches to reversing heart disease, such as Dr Dean Ornish's famous low-fat programme and the latest views about homocysteine. In place of the fad diets promising miracle cures, or the rigid dietary regimes that cut out virtually all fat, we offer a practical Healthy Heart programme that the entire family can follow.

For this latest volume, thanks are due to Dr John Mansfield, for his information on homocysteine, WDDTY columnist Harald Gaier, Contributing Editor Pat Thomas, particularly for her work on heart attacks, strokes, new diets and vegetarianism, and Production Editor Joanna Goldberg for helping to collate a mountain of material.

Lynne McTaggart

THE MYTH
OF PREVENTION

CHAPTER 1

THE CHOLESTEROL CONTROVERSY

Despite modern medicine's decided shortcomings in the treatment of existing illness, we are led to believe that doctors have enough understanding of our bodies to eradicate illness even before it's begun. Increasingly, doctors have turned their hand to what they like to call "preventive" medicine—that is, dispensing "just-in-case" medicine while you're still healthy to supposedly stop disease before it starts.

And ever since coronary heart disease moved into first place as a major killer in the West, scientists have once again been busy concocting and testing prevention theories. Epidemiologists are diligently collecting their statistics to examine the factors associated with an increased probability of developing the disease—the so-called risk factors.

In the 1960s, doctors first hypothesised that lowering blood cholesterol levels—either by drugs or by limiting fat intake—could prevent heart attacks and strokes. This in turn has led to an entire industry devoted to screening for high blood cholesterol and lowering it through processed, low-fat foods and the avoidance of many healthy foods, such as eggs. For 30 years, everyone in the Western world has been obsessed with fat. Young patients in the US and the UK have been roped into life-long medication regimes if screening tests showed a high cholesterol level. In the UK, between 1986 and 1992, the number of prescriptions for cholesterol-lowering drugs increased sixfold (BMJ, 1993; 306: 1367-73).

Cholesterol is itself a fat, or lipid, that is produced by the liver from the saturated fat in our diet. Some of it is absorbed directly from cholesterol-rich foods, such as egg yolks and dairy products, but the total amount of saturated fat eaten is of overall importance. Cholesterol is an important "building block" of life, a component of every single one of our cells. Blood cholesterol consists of low-density lipoprotein cholesterol (LDL), very low-density lipoprotein cholesterol (VLDL) and high-density lipoprotein cholesterol (HDL).

Both LDL and VLDL are regarded as the real culprits in heart disease, while HDL actually protects against heart disease by drawing cholesterol away from the lining of arteries. Nobody in medicine really knows just what constitutes a dangerous level of blood cholesterol, but doctors generally consider a total cholesterol count exceeding 5.2 mmol/l as the threshold for ordering in one or another armaments of intervention.

Despite the rapid development of an entire cholesterol-reducing industry, we have never actually been able to prove a cause-and-effect relationship between cholesterol and heart disease. Heart attack victims are *assumed* to have a high blood cholesterol levels and a high cholesterol count is *assumed* to be the cause of hardened arteries. From there, modern medicine has made the giant logical leap that a high dietary cholesterol intake causes a high blood cholesterol level and sets off a chain of events leading to a heart attack.

In fact, cholesterol lowering may be one of the biggest red herrings of the century. After 30 years or more of this "preventive" medicine, evidence is emerging that neither cholesterol-lowering drugs nor many of the recommended low-cholesterol diets help at all in preventing heart disease, and might actually increase your chances of dying. Many of the regimes recommended by medicine may, in fact, be among the main culprits in causing heart disease. Nor has any cholesterol-lowering drug been shown capable of lowering overall mortality rates over time; in many cases, the number of heart attacks may have dropped, but deaths from heart problems have not lowered significantly and overall deaths caused by other factors have risen.

There is ample scientific evidence suggesting that cholesterol may not even be the main cause of heart disease. One study involving nearly 20,000 men and women from Copenhagen demonstrated that only those with cholesterol blood levels in the top 5 per cent were at risk of developing heart disease (BMJ, 1994; 309: 11-15). Indeed, the staggering fact of it is *that most heart patients actually have normal cholesterol levels* (Lancet, 1994; 344: 1182-6).

Although many small studies have been suggesting it for some time, the most comprehensive of heart research studies concluded that cholesterol cannot be considered to be the only cause of coronary disease.

In the 1950s, the Seven Countries Study was established to try to understand the causes of heart disease. After collating their data, gleaned over 25 years, the researchers had to conclude that the risks involved a complex mix of factors, including cholesterol, smoking, high blood pressure and, most especially, diet. The importance of diet was reflected by the marked difference in heart-disease incidence in different countries (JAMA, 1995; 274: 131-6).

Many populations with high levels of heart disease don't have correspondingly high levels of fat in their diets. For instance, a group of Dutch researchers travelled to Minsk (Belarus), an area with unusually high rates of heart disease, and took fatty tissue samples from a group of men and women who'd been hospitalised for minor problems. Upon analysing the fat samples, the researchers found no evidence that the Minsk sample contained unusually high levels of saturated fats or unusually low levels of essential fatty acids (EFAs), both considered risk factors for heart disease. They concluded that dietary fat probably wasn't the major cause of heart disease in that area (Lancet, 1994; 344: 963-4).

Other research also suggests that we've been fingering the wrong culprit. One study discovered that the root of the problem was not cholesterol so much as the blood-clotting factor fibrinogen. Men with fibrinogen levels in the top fifth were four times more likely to suffer from heart disease than those with levels in the bottom fifth. Smokers, apparently, have high levels of fibrinogen, which confirms the long-held concern about the link between smoking and heart attacks. Yet further research lays the blame on high levels of homocysteine, an amino acid (Lancet, 1995; 345: 882).

The latest theory proposes that your biggest risk factor is a low melatonin level. Doctors from the University of Vienna found that people with a heart problem tend to produce lower levels of this hormone at night. Normally, healthy people release melatonin while sleeping, which tends to stop or slow the activity of the endocrine glands. These glands affect growth and metabolism (Lancet, 1995; 345: 1408).

Whether this or anything else proves to be the new "risk" factor or just the latest red herring, the fact remains that cholesterol hasn't been proven a risk factor for anything. A major US study discovered that neither high nor low cholesterol levels seem to have any bearing on any of the major illnesses, including heart disease and cancer. Researchers from the University of Southern California, who analysed some 2000 deaths among a group of 7000 middle-aged men of Japanese descent, concluded that early deaths were caused by a multitude of risk factors, but never cholesterol on its own (JAMA, 1995; 273: 1926-32).

Even among elderly patients, who would logically seem to be at higher risk, the link between high cholesterol levels and heart disease has failed to materialise. Higher total cholesterol levels have been associated with longevity in people over 85 years, who were also less likely to die from cancer or infection (Lancet, 1997; 350: 1119-23). Another study followed a large sample of patients over 70 for four years. A high cholesterol level didn't put them at a greater risk of dying from anything, including heart disease, heart attack or unstable angina (JAMA, 1994; 272: 1335-40).

For women, a low-fat diet may actually increase their risk of heart disease. In one group of 15,000 Scottish women, those with higher levels of cholesterol than men were shown to be less likely to die from heart disease than men with the highest levels. Lowering a woman's cholesterol levels also seems to lower her levels of HDL, the "good" form of cholesterol (Daily Telegraph, 16 April 1993).

Drugs to lower cholesterol

Regardless of sex, past evidence has suggested that the number of people likely to benefit from cholesterol-lowering drugs is small. In one study, only those at very high initial risk of coronary heart disease were likely to benefit. For those at medium risk, the drugs made no difference, while those at lower risk were more likely to die if they were being treated than if they weren't (Daily Telegraph, 16 April 1993).

Although they may lower cholesterol levels over the short term, cholesterol drugs may not have any long-term value in preventing arterial disease. Even after years of taking simvastatin, a cholesterol-lowering drug, patients in a study conducted among a number of centres in Europe were no better off in preventing clogged arteries than if they'd never taken any drug (Lancet, 1994; 344: 633-8).

In a British Medical Journal editorial (1993; 306: 1355-6), Matthew G Dunnigan, consultant physician at Stobhill General Hospital in Glasgow, concluded that "the lack of evidence of significant reductions in all causes of mortality by lipid-lowering drugs, particularly in primary prevention trials, indicates that any favourable effect of lipid-lowering drugs on all causes of mortality is at best small and of only marginal benefit to the individual."

As this kind of evidence poured in, many doctors stepped forward to voice their concerns about the open floodgate of cholesterol-drug prescribing. Michael Oliver, director of the Wynn Institute for Metabolic Research of the National Heart and Lung Institute in London, emphasised that there was a decided lack of evidence in all the major studies performed to date that any drugs were saving lives (BMJ, 1992; 304: 393-4; 431-4).

This mounting scepticism among doctors was virtually swept aside in late 1994 by the publication and subsequent publicity of a single trial, the Scandinavian Simvastatin Survival Study, which appeared to vindicate cholesterol-lowering drugs, at least among patients with a heart condition and high cholesterol levels. Dubbed the 4S study, it followed 4,444 patients with a heart condition and high cholesterol levels. After five and a half years, the group given cholesterol drugs had a 42 per cent lower rate of fatal heart attacks and a one-third reduction in heart disease over those given a placebo (Lancet, 1994; 344: 1383-9). Women in the group did not enjoy the same improved survival statistics. Although only a fifth of the study population were women, the mortality rate in the female placebo group was half of what it was for the placebo-taking men, suggesting that high cholesterol levels may be a meaningless indicator of future heart disease in women.

Within a week, the medical press was back on the cholesterol bandwagon, proclaiming, "Simvastatin saves lives" (Monitor Weekly, 30 Nov 1994: 17). Michael Brown and Joseph Goldstein, the 1985 Nobel prize winners for their work on cholesterol, praised the "landmark" results and endorsed the "definitive answer" provided by the Scandinavian study.

Hard at the heels of the 4S research was the West of Scotland

Coronary Prevention Study (WOSCOPS). This study purported to show that pravastatin, another "statin" cholesterol-lowering drug, could prevent heart attacks by a third in men with high levels of cholesterol but no history of heart disease (New Eng J Med, 1995; 333: 1301-7). Other studies, including one review of all studies of pravastatin, have concluded that this drug could reduce the rate of heart attacks by at least 60 per cent and could slow hardening of the arteries (Circulation, 1995; 92: 2419-25; J Am College Cardio, 1995; 26: 1133-9).

Although there were many important differences between these trials, the effect that these conclusions had on the medical rank and file was galvanic. The WOSCOP study was widely interpreted to mean that otherwise healthy men with high cholesterol levels could take cholesterol drugs to reduce their chances of dying of heart disease by nearly a third. All patients with higher cholesterol levels, irrespective of age or sex, were being placed on cholesterol-lowering drugs for life (Lancet, 1996; 347: 1267-8). One hospital in Dundee, which maintained records of the cholesterol drugs prescribed before and after the 4S study was published, found a striking increase both in the percentage of patients whose cholesterol was being measured (by a third) and in the percentage of patients being prescribed drugs (by nearly eight times) (Lancet, 1996; 347: 551-2). Many of these recipients of cholesterol-lowering drugs were elderly or female, despite the fact that neither of these patient groups had been thoroughly studied. Even though the 4S study showed limited benefit of cholesterol-lowering drugs for women, and women weren't even included in WOSCOPS, more than half of all cholesterol patients now receiving drugs in the US are, in fact, women (Lancet, 1996; 347: 1389-90).

Only a few brave dissidents have questioned the design of the 4S study and have voiced what they consider a number of basic flaws. For one thing, anyone with coronary heart disease was admitted into the study, regardless of whether or not his illness was caused by hardened arteries. In the drug-treatment group, 38 people had already undergone bypass surgery or angioplasty by the time they entered the study, and were therefore less likely to die. There were also 54 more smokers in the control group than in the treatment group, which just may have had something to do with their greater mortality rate (Lancet, 1995; 345: 264).

William Stehbens, a pathologist of the Wellington School of Medicine in New Zealand, pointed out that in the 4S study, the actual difference in death rate between the two groups from all causes was only 3.3 per cent. Stehbens also notes that the control group took a placebo containing methyl-cellulose, which causes tissue storage in arteries when given intravenously to rabbits—a condition that sounds not dissimilar to the effect of atherosclerosis.

In the WOSCOP study, deaths from heart disease among those not given the cholesterol-lowering drug were more than that of the general population—closer to the average death rate in people at least 10 years older—suggesting that particular people selected to represent the "average citizen" happened to be more ill than usual (Lancet, 1996; 347: 1267-8). Furthermore, although pravastatin did reduce cholesterol levels and deaths from heart attacks in the WOSCOPS, it did not significantly save lives from other coronary disease or any other cause.

A review of all studies on pravastatin also failed to show that a reduction in heart attacks translated into a significant number of lives being saved. Any improvements in the death rate, other than from heart attacks, were not considered statistically significant (Journal Watch, 1995; 15: 181-2; 190). And even if you tally in the survivals from heart attacks, overall survival over five years in the WOSCOPS trial was only increased from 96 to 97 per cent with the drug, and in the 4S trial from 87.7 to 91.3 per cent (New Eng J Med, 1996; 334: 1333-4). Nonetheless, many people with no history of heart attack may be put on cholesterol-lowering drugs indefinitely for an extremely minimal gain.

There remains a great deal we still do not know about cholesterol-lowering drugs. Patients are being counselled to take statins indefinitely, even though these drugs have not been tested in the elderly. And we don't know what effects these drugs have on someone who takes them over many years (Lancet, 1996; 347: 1389-90).

Some researchers also have noted that slightly more people died from all other causes in the 4S study. Although this number wasn't considered statistically significant, such a finding means we need more studies into whether cholesterol-lowering drugs could be responsible for increasing deaths from other causes (Lancet, 1995; 346: 1440-1). So far, we do know that a low blood cholesterol concentration can cause haemorrhagic stroke (BMJ, 1994; 308: 373-9).

Few have paused to consider the financial implications of long-term cholesterol prescribing. If WOSCOPS showed a 2.2 per cent prevention in heart attack, this means that 143 men with high cholesterol levels must be treated for five years to prevent one death from a cardiovascular cause. In the US, pravastatin costs $100 for a month's supply, or $6000 for each patient for those five years; $858,000 worth of cholesterol-lowering drugs need to be consumed in order to prevent perhaps one death. Since middle-aged women have only about a fourth the incidence of heart disease as men, it may cost as much as $3.4 million to prevent the death from heart disease of one woman (New Eng J Med, 1996; 334: 1333). And if we're talking about only mildly elevated cholesterol, the number of people you need to treat to prevent just one heart attack goes up even more (Lancet, 1996; 347: 1267-8).

Violent deaths
The biggest problem with patients on cholesterol-lowering programmes is that they become more likely to die from causes other than heart disease. In the early nineties, a number of large-

scale studies emerged revealing that patients on cholesterol diets or drugs were more likely to die from violent deaths, including suicide, than those who were just eating what they wanted (BMJ, 1992; 304: 431-3). This bizarre connection was dismissed as a quirk until it was confirmed by a number of subsequent international studies.

Research from Italy confirmed that low cholesterol levels do indeed tend to make people suicidal. The blood levels of 300 people who'd attempted suicide were compared with those of an identical number of people who'd never tried to harm themselves. In virtually all cases, the suicide group had lower levels of cholesterol close to the time they attempted suicide (BMJ, 1995; 310: 1632-6).

The most recent research has revealed that men with low cholesterol levels are up to three times more likely to commit suicide. Among 6,393 Parisians studied, scientists discovered that men with low cholesterol levels were 3.16 times more likely to commit suicide, while those whose cholesterol levels fell by more than 0.13 mmol/l a year were 2.17 times at greater risk (BMJ, 1996; 313: 649-64). Those with naturally low levels are at greatest risk, but men whose cholesterol levels are lowered with drugs also ran a risk, doubling their likelihood of suicide.

In 1992, Dr Hyman Engelberg of the Department of Medicine at Cedars-Sinai Medical Center in Los Angeles proposed that the link between the increase in violent deaths and cholesterol lowering was actually due to a reduction in serotonin (Lancet, 1992; 339: 727-9). One of the functions of this hormone in the central nervous system is to suppress our harmful behavioural impulses, such as aggression. In animal studies, mice with lowered cholesterol also had a decrease in the number of serotonin receptors in their brains (Lancet, 1993; 341: 75-9). As Engelberg concludes: "A lowered serum cholesterol concentration may contribute to a decrease in brain serotonin, with poor suppression of aggressive behaviour."

Interestingly, one effect of the new class of antidepressant drugs—selective serotonin re-uptake inhibitors (SSRI), such as fluoxetine (Prozac)—is to block serotonin from reaching certain cells in the nervous system. Numerous instances of violent or suicidal tendencies among patients taking these drugs have been reported.

Researchers from the University of California at San Diego found that depression was three times more common in patients over 70 with low blood cholesterol than in those with higher levels. What's more, the researchers found that the extent of depression correlated with the level of cholesterol: the lower the cholesterol, the more depressed the patient (Lancet, 1993; 341: 75-9).

This problem may only occur among older people, since there has never been any evidence of a relationship among younger people between violence and drugs taken to control cholesterol levels. But we do have some evidence that people on weight-loss programmes have significantly reduced levels of tryptophan—the essential amino acid that serotonin is mainly derived from—in their blood, as well as significant changes in their levels of serotonin (Psychol Med, 1990; 20: 785-91). We get tryptophan from certain foods, mainly proteins, and dietary supplements. When the diets of several countries are compared, those with low tryptophan intake have a higher rate of suicide. We also have evidence that patients suffering from severe depression have low levels of tryptophan and feel even worse if they are put on low-tryptophan diets. As their depression improves, so do their levels of tryptophan (M Werbach, *Nutritional Influences on Mental Illness*, Tarzana, CA: Third Line Press, 1991: 145-9).

Although other evidence has shown a greater risk of suicide, the higher the level of cholesterol (Arch Intern Med, 1995; 155: 695-700), another overview trial failed to find an association (BMJ,

1995; 311: 807). The answer may have something to do with all the changes in our diet over the last century, which have altered the ratio of the two types of EFAs, with a decrease in omega-3 fatty acids, such as are found in fatty fish and flaxseed oil, and an increase in the omega-6 fatty acids in polyunsaturated oils. When this ratio is altered (as it would be for either a high- or low-fat diet), patients have been shown to have increased levels of depression (Am J Clin Nutri, 1995; 62: 1-9).

Whatever the association, it's obvious that medicine doesn't yet understand the delicate interrelation of hormonal messages that the brain receives, or the dietary requirements necessary to sustain them. All your doctor's well-intended advice may be creating a good deal more havoc than the very worst Western diet.

Unsafe drugs

Besides the possibility of violent death, cholesterol drugs have been deemed unsafe for other reasons. Many doctors stopped prescribing clofibrate (Atroid), following a World Health Organisation (WHO) trial showing that it increased the mortality rate among heart patients by 44 per cent. The death rate only returned to normal once the drug was withdrawn (Brit Heart J, 1978; 40: 1069-118).

Questran (cholestyramine), another drug routinely prescribed to lower cholesterol levels, can cause constipation, flatulence, heartburn, nausea, diarrhoea, stomach upsets, skin rashes and, rarely, fat in the faeces. It can also lead to vitamin K deficiency which may cause increased bleeding due to the inability of the blood to clot properly. In animal studies, cholestyramine has been linked with intestinal cancer (*Physicians' Desk Reference*, Montvale, NJ: Medical Economics Data Production Company, 1995: 710-12). Even cases of sexual dysfunction have been reported in patients taking gemfibrozil, another cholesterol-lowering drug. Margaret from Surrey was on Zocor (simvastatin) for 18 months. She says she never would have taken it had her doctor told her about its side effects:

> *When I complained to my doctor about these effects, he dismissed them. To my complaint about dry mouth, for example, he said that I did not drink enough water. Nosebleeds, which I'd never had before, brought no comment from him, other than that I should see an ear, nose and throat surgeon to have my nose cauterised.*
>
> *A cardiologist helped me to get my blood pressure down, which corrected the extreme breathlessness I had been experiencing. But since starting on Zocor, increased breathlessness practically immobilised me—at the least bit of exertion! Even though I stopped taking the drug in August, my severe itching continues.*
>
> *Recently, I saw an advertisement about a similar cholesterol drug in a magazine. In the fine print, the ad clearly states some of the side effects that I've suffered. Why has my doctor never considered that Zocor could be the cause of my problems?*

As Margaret rightly points out, dry mouth, shortness of breath, blood-clotting problems and itching are but a few of the host of side effects from cholesterol-lowering drugs—including, in some cases, the risk of a heart attack.

The latest suspicion is that cholesterol-lowering drugs used over the long term may even cause cancer. Cholesterol policy expert Dr Thomas Newman of the University of California at San Francisco and his colleague Dr Stephen Hulley analysed the data published in the American drug reference bible, the *Physicians' Desk Reference*, plus population studies of cancer and cholesterol levels, and clinical trials of cholesterol lowering. They discovered a definite link between some of the popular cholesterol-lowering drugs and a risk of cancer.

Tests carried out on rodents clearly show the carcinogenic effects of some of these drugs, especially if taken over the long term. In Britain, gemfibrozil, marketed as Lopid, has been linked to tumour growth in mice and rats, but only when the animals are given 10 times the recommended dose per day. Although other drugs have been shown to cause cancer in animals without posing a threat to humans, Drs Newman and Hulley suggest that the doses of statin cholesterol-lowering drugs being taken by humans are comparable to the doses that have proved carcinogenic in these experimental animals (JAMA, 1996; 275: 55). *The ABPI Data Sheet Compendium*, the UK's drugs reference guide, reports a "significant increase" in liver cancer in rats given the overdose. Several cholesterol-lowering drugs have also been associated with lung, thyroid, testis and lymph node cancers (JAMA, 1996; 275: 1481-2).

Drs Newman and Hulley note that the drugs were approved by the US Food and Drug Administration (FDA) on the basis of less than 10 years' clinical trials. The full effects of the drugs may not become clear for another 30 years, particularly as many people are now being encouraged to take the drugs steadily over many decades.

The carcinogenic potential of two of the drugs, lovastatin and gemfibrozil, was discussed in a drugs advisory committee meeting of the FDA. But the drug manufacturer representative of lovastatin "downplayed the importance of the studies", maintain the California researchers. The data were also prepared in a way (milligrams per kilogram of body weight) which may have confused the committee.

Although they did approve the drugs, the FDA committee appears to have had reservations. Their original recommendation was to use gemfibrozil as a last resort, only after exercise, diet and weight control had failed to lower cholesterol levels. The popularity of the drug since then (use has increased ten-fold in the last decade, with 26 million prescriptions written in the US alone in 1992) suggests that its use has been far more widespread than the committee advised.

Although Newman and Hulley agree that extrapolating evidence of damage in rodents to humans is an uncertain business, they do not press for an all-out ban. They believe that the benefits of the drugs outweigh the risks among men with very high blood cholesterol who are at a short-term high risk of heart attacks—so long as they don't take the drug for more than five years. However, they feel that those who are not at high risk should avoid the drugs, particularly if they have a life expectancy greater than 20 years.

CHAPTER 2

HIGH BLOOD PRESSURE: DANGER IN NUMBERS

High blood pressure has been linked with strokes, kidney disease and, surprisingly, to a lesser degree with heart attacks. However, if your doctor tells you your blood pressure is high, that isn't cause for alarm. There's a fair likelihood that you've been misdiagnosed or even that your high blood pressure is not high at all for your age. Even with about 50 million Americans (one in four adults) and one in seven adults in Britain with hypertension, no one knows exactly what causes high blood pressure, although it does seem to be at least partially hereditary.

A crude piece of equipment

Both the premise on which a diagnosis of hypertension is made—any reading over 95 mmHg diastolic—and the equipment used to make the diagnosis are decidedly flawed. Normally, a blood pressure cuff, which consists of a rubber bag in a cloth sleeve, is wrapped around your upper arm. Air is pumped into the bag until its pressure is higher than the pressure in your arm's main artery, and this stops the flow of blood. Then, when the air is released from the cuff's bag, blood surges into the artery again; this is heard with a stethoscope placed over your arm's main artery. Systolic pressure is the point at which the doctor first hears blood forcing itself through the flattened artery, expanding it and causing the heart muscle to contract. The second, diastolic pressure, is the point at which the sound fades away, when the arteries are relaxed and filling the heart with blood. These readings are expressed as millimetres of mercury (mmHg)—a throwback to the days when doctors used to measure it with a glass column filled with mercury—and a reading of 120 mmHg systolic and 80 mmHg diastolic is written as 120/80.

Professor William White, chief of Hypertension and Vascular Diseases at the University of Connecticut, refers to the blood pressure cuff, known in medicalese as the "sphygmomanometer", as "medicine's crudest investigation". Blood pressure, he says, can fluctuate tremendously—as much as 30 mmHg over the course of any day, rising when we exercise or encounter stress, and falling when we relax or sleep (BMJ, 1991; 303: 120-1). In fact, the time when your blood pressure is most likely to rise is in your doctor's surgery, when you're waiting to have the test—a condition known as "white coat hypertension".

A mildly high blood pressure is even quite common and, because blood pressure rises as we age, it's normal if you're over 55. Despite what is usually considered a high level, a normal blood pressure for older people is somewhere around 140/90; this is comparable to a blood pressure level of around 120/80 in a healthy young woman. If you're over 50, some experts such as the American Health Research Group believe only a systolic level of 180 mmHg and over, and a diastolic level of 100 mmHg and over, should be treated.

Even the choice of which arm to cuff can influence a blood pressure reading. One doctor from City General Hospital in Staffordshire, England, discovered a variation of more than 8 mmHg in systolic blood pressure between the two arms of nearly a quarter of his patients. In one case, there was a 20 mmHg difference between arms (JAMA, 1995; 274: 1343).

Blood pressure measurements become even more confused for

pregnant women and children. Doctors and health care workers can't agree on how to record the diastole, or second beat of blood pressure, or whether certain sounds accurately reflect diastolic pressure (Lancet, 1991; 338: 130). In fact, this was the subject of a heated debate at a world congress of hypertension in pregnancy in Italy in 1990, which called for an "international consensus" on how to record blood pressure in pregnant women.

Recently, some researchers have even claimed that doctors have been using the wrong type of blood pressure test on pregnant women: obstetricians and midwives prefer the blood pressure gauge called Korotkoff phase 4, but new research shows that phase 5 testing is far more reliable—the reverse of the prevailing view. In one test, virtually nobody agreed on the reading from a K4 test, while everyone was in agreement on the K5 test (Lancet, 1996; 347: 139-42).

The potential for so many different interpretations of a blood pressure reading can cause problems if your blood pressure is being monitored by several people, who may have had different training in how to take measurements.

Yet another flaw in the blood pressure practice—the use of defective testing equipment—was exposed by a report in GP magazine (4 Jan 1993). A survey of 300 GPs by the London School of Tropical Medicine found that most were using equipment which falls below standards set by the British Hypertension Society. All too often, the cuffs being used were an average of 11 cm shorter than the recommended length for people who were lean or of average weight. A cuff that is too small will overstate a patient's blood pressure, giving inaccurate readings and unnecessary cause for alarm. Only 7 per cent of the respondents were actually aware of the correct cuff sizes.

These days, your doctor may be more likely to strap you up with a portable electronic device, which will measure your blood pressure at pre-set intervals over 24 hours. Taking a large number of measurements throughout the day and averaging them out should, in theory, give a doctor a better idea of your true blood pressure. But there is a great deal of evidence that even this system, called "ambulatory monitoring", cannot provide accurate enough information for doctors to decide whether a patient needs treatment for high blood pressure (BMJ, 1992; 305: 1062-6). There has been evidence, however, that patients whose blood pressure is measured in this way need fewer drugs than people whose blood pressure is monitored with the usual cuff (JAMA, 1997; 278: 1065-72).

The WHO now recommends that ambulatory monitoring is best conducted with multiple readings over six months. But because there have been no large scale scientific studies, no one can agree on how long to conduct ambulatory monitoring before making a diagnosis, what actually constitutes high blood pressure over this period, or even how much blood pressure should be lowered to make it "normal" (J Hypertension, 1994; 12: 857-66).

Drugs that cause hypertension

A load of other drugs, used to treat completely different conditions, can actually cause hypertension. Cyclosporine, a powerful immunosuppressant, can raise systolic blood pressure (Hypertension, 1994; 24: 480-5) and create arterial hypertension in heart transplant patients (J Human Hypertension, 1994; 8: 233-7). Kidney transplant patients often suffer from hypertension. Cyclosporine-associated hypertension appears to involve sodium retention and stimulates the sympathetic nervous system (Am J Kidney Diseases, 1994; 23: 471-5).

Patients taking medium and low doses of cyclosporine for severe psoriasis over three years have developed hypertension (Br J Dermatology, 1990; 123: 347-53). Indeed, it has been established that cyclosporine treatment can cause a patient to develop hypertension within a few weeks (Am J Hypertension,

1991; 4: 468-71).

Hypertension can even be a side effect from using oral contraceptives (Ceska Gynekologie, 1994; 59: 62-3). Insulin is also thought to raise blood pressure in diabetics, although this is currently under debate (Drugs, 1994; 47: 383-404).

Hydrocortisone raises blood pressure in men (Am J Hypertension, 1993; 6: 287-94), and non-steroidal anti-inflammatory drugs (NSAIDs), used to treat arthritis, can raise blood pressure in the elderly (Br J Clin Pharm, 1993; 35: 455-9).

Patients taking tricyclic antidepressants for panic disorders have suffered from hypertension (Am J Cardiology, 1992; 70: 1306-9). Desipramine increases pulse and blood pressure when used to treat sufferers of bulimia nervosa (J Clin Psychopharm, 1992; 12: 163-8), although blood pressure does come down over time.

Even nasal decongestants and cough syrup, if taken in large enough doses, can induce hypertension (DICP, 1991; 25: 1068-70).

Drugs for hypertension

Hypertension is an area where a mountainous concoction of drugs rarely does any good against a condition that can usually be solved with judicious diet and exercise. Doctors have ploughed through a variety of drug treatments without apparent success. A study of 2000 patients with high blood pressure from 13 general practices in England revealed that only a little more than half of those taking drugs for hypertension had achieved what is considered a moderately healthy level (Lancet, 1994; 344: 1019-20). Even the modest blood pressure goals set in the US Nutrition and Health Examination Survey—less than 140/90 mmHg—were reached in only a fifth of patients taking drugs in the US (Arch Intern Med, 1993; 153: 154-83). As for Europe, in a survey of 12,000 patients across five countries, only a third managed to achieve the blood pressure target set by their doctors (Blood Pressure, 1993; 2: 5-9).

Furthermore, most drugs are not only vastly overused but largely unnecessary for most mild cases of raised blood pressure. One study found that almost half of patients over 50 years old had normal blood pressure a year after being taken off hypertensive drugs. Many of these drugs should also be carefully avoided if you have asthma or diabetes.

GPs continue to throw drugs at a condition which may just as easily be cured naturally. They don't have enough time to consider a more effective diagnosis, they may have too many conditions to deal with, or they often don't have the sort of detailed therapeutic knowledge that may be required to treat high blood pressure effectively.

"Their basic education in therapeutics is sadly lacking," says Professor Peter Sever at St Mary's Hospital Medical School in London. "Historically, and now, therapeutics education at medical school is a tiny part of the curriculum. When you think it's such a major component of every GP's daily practice, there's a colossal imbalance there."

According to Professor Sever, GPs delude themselves into thinking they are treating blood pressure effectively when, in practice, they're not: "Their big decision is taken when they decide whether or not to start therapy, but once they've started their patients on a drug, they appear very reluctant to change," he says.

If there isn't much evidence that blood pressure drugs do a lot of good, there's plenty to show they do great harm. Some drugs, intended to cure hypertension, can actually exacerbate the condition. Others can kill you.

Beta-blockers, diuretics, reserpine, methyldopa and clonidine are usually prescribed for hypertension. These have all been implicated in various disorders, including depression, impotence and sexual dysfunction, loss of appetite, nausea and tiredness. One particularly worrisome side effect is hypotension—a sudden drop in blood pressure when one stands up—which can cause dizziness and falls. In fact, hypertensive drugs are the major cause of hip fractures among senior citizens (S M Wolfe, R E Hope, *Worse Pills, Best Pills, II,* Washington, DC: Public Citizens' Health Research Group, 1993: 10).

Traditionally, a diuretic (water pill) has usually been the doctor's first line of defence against high blood pressure. This supposedly "safe" blood pressure drug has, however, been shown to cause an 11-fold increase in diabetes (BMJ, 1994; 308: 855).

Beta-blockers

Diuretics are then often followed by the prescription of a beta-blocker, which works by blocking the effects of adrenaline on the beta receptors in the heart and arteries. This drug also reduces the heart's output and alters kidney function, affects the blood pressure control centre in the brain, and changes the sensitivity of blood pressure monitoring nerves.

Not surprisingly, any drug this powerful has some pretty potent side effects as well. These include dizziness, low blood pressure, low blood sugar, loss of appetite and nausea, impotence and sexual dysfunction, drowsiness, fatigue and depression. As for more long-range problems, this class of drugs can cause kidney and liver damage, Raynaud's syndrome (problems with blood supply to the hands and feet) and other mental changes, such as nightmares, hallucinations and insomnia.

It's also possible that the beta-blocker atenolol could be responsible for some cancer deaths among elderly hypertensive men (BMJ, 1993; 306: 609-11), although this is suspected to be a "chance observation"—whatever that means.

Yet in another study, atenol doubled the risk of kidney cancer in hypertensive patients (Hypertension, 1996; 28: 321-4)

Doctors have even used these drugs to treat women with hypertension during pregnancy, in spite of the fact that beta-blockers are thought to have a harmful effect on foetal circulation (BMJ, 1992; 304: 946-9).

Beta-blockers may even affect certain kinds of memory. A team at the University of California at Irvine divided a healthy group of volunteers into two sub-groups. One group was given propranolol and the other a placebo an hour before they were shown slides telling two stories. Physical tests taken just before these slide stories were shown demonstrated that all the drug-takers were fully beta-blocked.

The first story illustrated a child visiting his father's workplace with his mother. The second story, designed to arouse strong emotions, showed that the child was hit by a car and badly injured on the way to the workplace.

A week after seeing these images, when all the subjects were given a surprise memory test, both groups showed similar results when recounting the first story. However, the propranolol group had significantly worse recall of the second, emotionally charged story (Nature, 1994; 371: 702-4).

The study is limited in that it examined the effect of a single dose of beta-blocker on healthy subjects. Nevertheless, animal studies have demonstrated that memory of emotionally charged events requires activating the beta-adrenergic systems, which of course are blocked by beta-blocking drugs.

Bristol-Myers Squibb, which manufacturers the beta-blocker sotalol as Sotacor, warns that their drug may precipitate heart failure in subjects with a weak heart or may aggravate existing heart failure. It also should be used with caution on older subjects with potential kidney problems. The company further recommends that patients on this drug have their potassium levels monitored since sotalol has been known to cause "torsade de pointes", an unusually rapid heartbeat of more than 100 beats per minute. It should also not be used by diabetics (it can mask warning signs) or those with a history of bronchospasm.

Recently, researchers from the Ochsner Clinic in New Orleans analysed 10 trials which compared beta-blockers with diuretics.

They discovered that the elderly were more likely to suffer a sudden and fatal heart attack while taking beta-blockers. This class of drugs also wasn't particularly effective: less than one-third of the 2000 patients in one particular study had their high blood pressure effectively controlled by beta-blockers, compared with two-thirds who had theirs successfully treated with diuretics (JAMA, 1998; 279: 1903-7).

ACE inhibitors

ACE (angiotensin-converting enzyme) inhibitors, a class of drugs used to treat heart attack victims, are now replacing diuretics and beta-blockers as first-line treatments for high blood pressure. As the name implies, they work by blocking the action of angiotensin, the chemical in the blood which causes blood vessels to narrow, so that blood can flow more easily.

Evidence now suggests that inhibiting angiotensin may actually increase the risk of death if ACE inhibitors are given too soon after a heart attack. Researchers from Scandinavia (N Eng J Med, 1992; 327: 678-84) looked at coronary patients given the ACE inhibitor enalapril within 24 hours of a heart attack. The trial prematurely ended when it was discovered that those taking the drug were at increased risk of suffering from potentially fatal low blood pressure. Another study published the same year found no reduction in mortality among those with heart conditions but no symptoms given enalapril as a preventive (N Eng J Med, 1992; 327: 685-91).

The pharmaceutical giant Bristol-Myers Squibb funded a £6 million research study comparing the effectiveness of magnesium with the angiotensin-blocking drug captopril for people with heart problems. Covering 58,000 patients from 1,086 hospitals, the study found only marginal benefits from magnesium, whereas patients on captopril had a 7 per cent lower death rate after five weeks than patients on standard treatment (Lancet, 1995; 345:

669-85). When the results of this study were first announced, however, it was criticised by some heart specialists for being unreliable and enrolling unsuitable subjects. Captopril has also been suspected of lowering levels of bone marrow.

Perindopril is routinely prescribed for patients admitted with heart failure because it is thought not to affect blood pressure. But a 61-year-old man who was admitted to a Danish hospital for mild chest pain had his blood pressure levels fall so low as a result of perindopril that he suffered brain damage, which permanently damaged his vision (Lancet, 1997; 349: 1671-2).

ACE inhibitors have also been shown to cause potentially fatal kidney damage. Of 15 patients suffering kidney problems after taking the drugs, four became dependent on dialysis and died soon after and another five needed short-term dialysis (JAMA, 1993; 269: 1692).

If ACE inhibitors are used in the second and third trimesters of pregnancy, they can injure or kill the developing foetus (JAMA, 1992; 267: 2588).

The wide-ranging side effects of ACE inhibitors include swelling of the face, kidney failure, low white blood-cell count, abnormally high blood-potassium levels, nausea, diarrhoea, muscle weakness and, ironically, heart irregularities.

Calcium-channel blockers
Calcium-channel blockers are also being thrust into the front line. Increasingly, doctors have been prescribing these drugs over the past 10 years, even though their long-term benefits have never been validated by research.

The passage of calcium through special channels in the muscles of the heart is an important part of what makes the heart beat. Calcium-channel blockers prevent this movement of calcium by relaxing the blood-vessel muscles and thus encouraging them to dilate. This action helps reduce blood pressure and makes it easier for the heart to pump blood throughout the body.

However, these drugs also cause worrying side effects. For instance, diltiazem, a calcium-channel blocker used to treat hypertension and other heart problems, has been linked with severe skin disorders. Soon after a 42-year-old man was given the drug to treat high blood pressure, he began to develop skin lesions which developed into Stevens-Johnson Syndrome, with a rash across his whole body (Lancet, 1993; 341: 967).

Research from the University of Colorado has recently found that these drugs can also be dangerous for diabetics. In one study, patients with non-insulin-dependent diabetes who took the calcium-channel blocker nisoldipine were five times more likely to have a heart attack than those given enalapril maleate, an ACE inhibitor—despite the fact that the diabetics given ACE inhibitors had higher cholesterol levels to begin with (New Eng J Med, 1998; 338: 645-52).

Fears over the safety of calcium-channel blockers were further heightened when a Swedish study disclosed that people taking them were five times more likely to commit suicide than patients on other antihypertensive drugs (BMJ, 1998; 316: 741-5).

Other calcium-channel blockers, such as verapamil and nifedipine, are also used to treat hypertension. But the Food and Drug Administration (FDA) has now cautioned against using nifedipine since it has been shown to create first a sharp drop, followed five hours later by a sharp rise in blood pressure, thus increasing the risk of heart attack (JAMA, 1996; 275: 423; 515).

Nifedipine has been found to be the most dangerous of all the calcium-channel blockers (JAMA, 1995; 274: 620-5). American doctors have now been advised to stop prescribing the drug. The US National Heart, Lung and Blood Institute has warned doctors that short-acting nifedipine "should be used with great caution, if at all". The warning is based on the study of 16 scientific trials of short-acting nifedipine involving more than 8000 patients. The risk of dying increased with the dosage: the mortality risk is 1.06 times greater than normal with dosages of between 30 and 50 mg a day, and increases to nearly three times when the daily dose is 80 mg (Lancet, 1995; 346: 767-70; 586). One patient went completely blind 30 minutes after taking nifedipine tablets for high blood pressure (BMJ, 1992; 305: 693).

One of the studies examined by the Institute showed that patients taking calcium-channel blockers were 60 per cent more likely to suffer a heart attack than those taking either diuretics or beta-blockers.

More recently, researchers from the University of Washington in Seattle examined over 1000 men and women with hypertension over the age of 65. Those elderly patients taking calcium-channel blockers were found to have more white matter in the brain and to do poorer on a mental examination, compared with those taking beta-blockers (Lancet, 1997; 350: 1753).

Until recently, medical guidelines recommended that hypertension be treated with drugs if other non-drug solutions hadn't brought the blood pressure down below a specified level thought to be safe (Arch Intern Med, 1988; 148: 1023-38). However, little consideration was given to other factors that could significantly influence an individual's risk of hypertension-related disease.

A number of guidelines have now been published which reflect a new approach to treatment; they recognise that individuals suffering from a certain level of hypertension may not necessarily be candidates for heart trouble if their condition is based on blood pressure alone. Although hypertension is a major risk factor for heart disease, several other factors, such as smoking, obesity, diabetes, high cholesterol and lack of exercise, also contribute. Every patient is unique, so it makes no sense to treat each example of hypertension in the same way.

Guidelines issued by the WHO/International Society of

Hypertension (BMJ, 1993; 307: 1541-6) and the British Hypertension Society (BMJ, 1993; 306: 983-7) recommend that doctors take older age, other risk factors and potential organ damage into consideration when they're treating hypertensive patients. The American Joint National Committee (JNC) guidelines are less specific, but emphasise the importance of risk factors which can affect the heart and organs (Arch Intern Med, 1993; 153: 149-52).

Unfortunately, none of these spells out just how dangerous risk factors other than hypertension really are, although guidelines from New Zealand suggest that balancing the risk of treatment against the benefits is by no means a straightforward exercise (BMJ, 1993; 307: 107-10).

Effective care for patients suffering from hypertension all depends on how well doctors understand the whole patient. Non-pharmacological treatment plays an important part in any blood pressure-control programme, and should be offered to anyone with hypertension—whether they're taking drugs or not.

Weight

Body weight seems to affect blood pressure (BMJ, 1988; 297: 319-28) so losing weight naturally can lower blood pressure (New Eng J Med, 1978; 298: 1-6). Twenty-five to 30 per cent of all Americans are thought to be obese, and 20 per cent of men and 40 per cent of women are trying to lose weight at any one time (Lancet, 1994; 344: 307-11). A successful weight-reduction programme may reduce or completely remove the need for antihypertensive drugs, as well as improve quality of life.

A four-year regimen of losing just an average of 7.9 lbs (3.6 kg), drinking one glass of alcohol less a week, and introducing a diet low in cholesterol and fats has been shown to significantly lower blood pressure (JAMA, 1996; 275: 1549-56). It's particularly important for cardiac patients who are advised to stop smoking to take steps to avoid gaining an inordinate amount of weight.

Exercise

Mild aerobic exercise is an effective, drug-free way to reduce blood pressure (Lancet, 1993; 341: 1248-9), but has received less attention than other methods, such as losing weight and cutting down your intake of alcohol and sodium. Numerous relaxation techniques and methods of stress management, such as transcendental meditation, yoga, autogenic training and even hypnosis are all useful tools for lowering blood pressure.

Diet for hypertension

According to British nutritional expert Dr Stephen Davies, many cases of high blood pressure can be controlled by diet. Even some of the more conventional doctors agree that diet plays a significant role in hypertension.

The first and well established point is to exclude additional salt from your diet and avoid salty foods (Klinische Wochenschrift, 1991; 69: 17-25). A double cheeseburger alone contains around 150 per cent of your daily recommended intake of sodium—so be aware of the salt content of what you eat.

What is less well known is the role that potassium plays in helping to control blood pressure. Certain studies have suggested that individuals with a higher dietary intake of potassium have a lower incidence of stroke (New Eng J Med, 1987; 316: 235-40). A study at the University of Poona in India investigated whether potassium supplements, alone or in combination with magnesium, gave any benefit to patients with slightly elevated blood pressure. The researchers found that blood pressure lowered dramatically in patients taking the potassium supplements, while adding magnesium seemed to offer no additional benefit (BMJ, 15 Sept l990).

Several mass epidemiological surveys have also suggested that the less potassium in a person's diet, the more likely he is to suffer from hypertension—which may explain why vegetarians, whose

42

diet is more often rich in potassium, have a lower incidence of the disease than the population at large. However, much of the potassium that is naturally present in vegetables is lost in the cooking water if boiled for long periods of time. So for anyone with high blood pressure, it's a good idea to steam or only lightly cook vegetables, as well as to regularly eat raw potassium-rich foods, such as bananas.

There has also been some research into the role that calcium and magnesium play in hypertension, most of which indicates a link between low levels of these two elements and heart problems of all varieties. In a study involving 655 men aged between 45 and 59 years, researchers found that those suffering ischaemic heart disease had a daily magnesium intake 12 per cent lower than those with no heart symptoms (Lancet, 1992; 340: 483). Although magnesium and calcium supplements are believed to help reduce blood pressure, their case has not yet been proven (Am J Med, 1993; 93: 115-205; Am J Hypertension, 1990; 3: 1565-1605).

Other possible sources of high blood pressure could be a diet high in refined sugar, saturated fats, and tea and coffee. Two cups of coffee a day can raise your blood-pressure levels temporarily, and many believe that the effects of heavy caffeine consumption over a long period could do the same, particularly in men (Int J Psychophysiology, Dec 1990; BMJ, 1 March 1990). Drinking caffeine when under stress has also been found to raise blood pressure in young men (Health Psychology, 1991; 10: 236-43).

Besides limiting your consumption of coffee and tea, it's also a good idea to cut down on your intake of animal fats. In several studies, vegetarians generally had lower blood pressure than meat-eaters. Some quarters believe that it may be what many vegetarians include rather than exclude from their diet—more fibre, fruits, vegetables and whole grains—that keeps their blood pressure in check.

It is also important to eat less saturated fat while increasing your intake of essential fatty acids (EFAs). This means using quality polyunsaturated or monounsaturated cooking oils whenever possible. Fish oil reduces blood pressure in those whose levels are raised (Circulation, 1993; 88: 523-33), but doesn't appear to affect blood pressure levels in those not suffering from hypertension. Nevertheless, the higher the doses of fish oil, the greater the reduction in blood pressure—a fact that strengthens the case for a cause-and-effect relationship.

A more major, recent study involving 11,000 survivors of heart attacks has found that those who regularly take omega-3 fish oil supplements significantly reduce their chances of suffering a second attack or a stroke. Researchers from this GISSI-Prevenzione study in Italy gave survivors either fish oil supplements, vitamin E, both or nothing. After three-and-a-half years, 12.4 per cent of those who took fish oil suffered a second heart attack, stroke or death, compared with 13.7 per cent of those who did not (Lancet, 1999; 353: 988).

Although a little alcohol every day can actually lower your blood pressure, it's a good idea to restrict your intake to no more than one drink a day. Drinking heavily will increase the risk of hypertension (Hypertension, 1991; 18: 819-26; Orvosi Hetilap, 1991; 132: 63-4; 67-8). In fact, excessive alcohol consumption accounts for 5 to 30 per cent of all cases of hypertension (Hypertension, 1982; 4: 143-150). Beer containing tyramine (the darker the beer, the more tyramines it has) can also contribute to the condition, although moderate consumption should not affect your risk (J Clin Psychopharm, 1994; 14: 5-14).

Blood-pressure levels have been shown to decline for those eating a diet rich in fruits, vegetables and low-fat dairy foods. Hypertension patients who were given this diet had systolic and diastolic pressure rates lower 5.5 and 3 mmHg more than the blood pressure of controls (New Eng J Med, 1997; 336: 1117-24).

According to Dr Stephen Davies, other substances which can

raise blood pressure include the Pill, liquorice, toxic minerals like lead and cadmium, and some of the NSAIDs.

Lead, high levels of which are known to contribute to hypertension, dissolves much more easily in soft water. So, if you live in a soft water area, you have a higher risk of becoming hypertensive. Those who have had lead poisoning in childhood are also more likely to suffer from hypertension later in life (Am J Diseases Children, 1991; 145: 681-7).

CHAPTER 3

STROKE:
TAKE TWO ASPIRIN?

Often without warning, life can be torn apart by the sudden trauma to the brain caused by a stroke. The third biggest killer in the West, strokes are the most important cause of adult disability (Lancet, 1992; 339: 342-4). Among those over 65, it is the second most common cause of death after heart disease.

Stroke is a non-specific, collective term for symptoms, such as paralysis, perceptual loss, speech difficulties and visual problems, which are the result of damage to the brain tissue, caused by one of three means. Most commonly, a blood clot gradually builds up in a brain artery (arterial occlusion), eventually blocking the blood supply to a certain part of the brain (infarction). Starving this area of oxygen, cerebral thrombosis will leave its victim with a certain degree of tissue death. This can also be the result of atherosclerosis, or narrowing of the arteries. Often, both atherosclerosis and arterial occlusion are present together since the formation of blood clots in the brain can be the result of platelets forming in response to the damaged lining of the blood vessels. In the West, 85 per cent of strokes are a result of cerebral infarction from blood clots (Lancet, 1992; 339: 533-6).

Blockages in the brain, or cerebral embolism, may also be due to a clot which originated elsewhere in the body—usually in the heart or the deep veins in the legs—and travels upward. The third problem which could cause a stroke is a cerebral haemorrhage, where a blood vessel in the brain ruptures and the bleeding damages that area of the brain. High blood pressure can lead to haemorrhage, usually through an aneurysm—a local "ballooning" of an artery which causes it to burst. The extreme force of blood leaking from an artery damages the delicate brain tissue as well as compressing and impairing the function of adjacent tissues.

The degree of disability and loss of basic physical or mental skills after a stroke depends largely on the duration and the site of the trauma.

No disorder is more confounding to medical science since stroke cannot be pinned down to one single, treatable cause. Instead, it is influenced by a number of different factors—organic and iatrogenic. As a result, stroke prevention often takes a rather haphazard course and, in spite of vast amounts of money which have been poured into the study of stroke and related vascular disorders, there is still very little known about this devastating disorder (BMJ, 1995; 311: 139-40).

Much of the research concerns itself with finding the single most effective preventive for strokes, the most popular options being anticoagulants, antiplatelets, antihypertensives, diuretics and surgery. All too often, treatment ends up being a combination of any or all of these things.

It is also important to note that "effective" in stroke research generally means "cost effective", and that prevention is usually aimed at reducing the cost of patients requiring hospital admission and treatment for stroke, rather than improving their quality of life (JAMA, 1995; 274: 1839-45).

Women and stroke

The perception among physicians and the public is that stroke and heart disease are disorders affecting men, usually elderly men (New Eng J Med, 1991, 325: 274-6). Although in middle age the death rate from coronary heart disease is five times higher for men than women, in old age the rates become similar—heart disease is the leading cause of death for women as well as men.

Women live longer than men and comprise 64 per cent of the population over the age of 75 (JAMA, 1992; 268: 1417-22). Yet women and those over 65 are often excluded from research into heart disease and stroke. Several of the most well known research projects into cardiovascular disease have not included women (Women and Health Research, National Academy Press, 1994). Older people and women are often passed over by researchers because they complicate things: older people may have other health problems and may be taking other medicines which would interfere with the "purity" of a study's findings; women have a different chemical make-up from the male "gold standard".

Women in particular are at risk of stroke from an increased number of medical causes. For instance, it has long been known that the contraceptive pill increases the likelihood of stroke. A low-dose pill (50 mcg of oestrogen) can treble a woman's risk of thromboembolism (BMJ, 1996; 312: 83-8; Lancet, 1995; 346: 1375-82). Hormone replacement therapy carries a similar risk. According to American research, women taking drugs for heart conditions run a greater risk of developing torsades de pointes (JAMA, 1 Dec 1993).

There may also be a gender bias in the way women are treated for heart disease (New Eng J Med, 1991; 325: 129-35; 221-5). Women are less likely to be offered surgery and more likely to be offered drugs (thrombolytics, diuretics, antiplatelets) for treatment of heart disease, and these have been shown to increase the likelihood of a fatal stroke.

Drugs that cause strokes
A number of classes of drugs can cause cerebral haemorrhage or infarction. These include:

- Sumatripan, the migraine drug (Intensive Care Med, 1995; 21: 82-3).
- Beta-blockers (Revist Clinica Espan, 1993; 192: 228-30).
- Nifedipine (causing cortical blindness) (BMJ, 1992; 305: 693).
- Chemotherapy or hormones given during chemotherapy (Am J Clin Onc, 1992; 15: 168-73).
- All hormones, such as HRT and the Pill (Acta Neurol Belg, 1992; 92: 45-7).
- Oral anticoagulant therapy (Lancet, 1991; 338: 1158).
- Excessive use of nasal decongestants (J Neurol, Neurosurg Psychiatry; 1989; 52: 541-3).
- Blood-pressure-lowering drugs (Med J Australia, 1987; 146: 412-4).
- Phenylpropanolamine, a drug available over the counter in weight loss, nasal decongestants and cold preparations (Am J Emerg Med, 1987; 5: 163-4).
- Recreational drugs, like Ecstasy, cocaine and methamphetamines (European Neuro, 1995; 35: 193; South Med J, 1995; 88: 352-4; Europ Neuro, 1994; 34: 16-22).
- Anabolic steroids (Neuro, 1994; 44: 2405-6).

Clot-thinning medication for stroke and thrombosis can itself cause stroke. This includes:
- Streptokinase/subcutaneous heparin therapy, combination therapy (Circulation, 1995; 92: 2811-8) and recombinant tissue-type plasminogen activator (Circulation; 1991; 83: 448-59).
- Anti-coagulant medication (Arch of Neuro, 1985; 42: 1033-5).

Stroke can also be brought on by:
- Ingesting hydrogen peroxide (Stroke; 1994; 25: 1065-7).
- Lumbar myelography (Nervenarzt, 1994; 65: 125-7).
- Heavy drinking in men (Stroke; 1996; 27: 1033-9).

When thrombolysis—the use of drugs to dissolve blood clots—is used after cerebral infarction, the likely result is another stroke—this time caused by cerebral haemorrhage. Heparin and warfarin are both indicated in increased incidence of cerebral haemorrhage, but the most recent debate has been over the use of agents such as streptokiniase (SK) and recombinent tissue plasminogen activator (rtPA).

Three large SK trials have been terminated because of early high mortality due to intracerebral haemorrhage. One trial for rtPA also showed increased mortality. None of these four trials showed any improvement in disability that could offset the early mortality (Lancet, 1996; 347: 391).

Thrombolysis is a high-risk strategy in stroke, especially if administered "late" (three to six hours after the stroke). The National Institutes of Neurological Disorders and Stroke (NINDS) trial showed an even smaller "therapeutic window" (under three hours) for the administration of rtPA (New Eng J Med, 1995; 333: 1581-7).

The MAST-I trial (Lancet, 1995; 346: 1509-14) was abandoned when high death rates were revealed among those receiving these drugs. Mortality was increased from 24.3 per cent to 35.8 per cent in the first six months, though disability over the long term decreased from 53.4 per cent to 41.8 per cent.

Commentary on the trial questioned, among other things, whether it was ethical to ask patients if they would rather be dead or disabled (Lancet, 1995; 347: 391-3). The MAST-I results were not unique (Circulation, 1995; 92: 2811-8; New Eng J Med, 1995; 335: 1581-7; New Eng J Med, 1996; 336: 145-60).

Different thrombolytic drugs given in different ways may have different effects (JAMA, 1995; 274: 1017-25)—and it is the elderly—the majority of stroke patients—who are more likely to experience cerebral haemorrhage and have a higher mortality rate (Circulation, 1995; 92: 2811-8).

Take two aspirin?

The "magic bullet" philosophy upon which modern medicine is built does not benefit stroke patients. Perhaps the best example of this can be seen in the wholesale administration of aspirin—an antiplatelet—as both treatment and preventative for stroke. Aspirin not only thins the blood but also has an antihypertensive effect. For many physicians it has long seemed a logical way of preventing stroke in patients with constricted blood vessels, in those who have suffered heart attacks or in those who have experienced transient ischaemic attacks, or TIAs—minor strokes of short duration. The fact that it was cheap, readily available and familiar to patients was also in its favour.

Evidence for the use of aspirin in the treatment of stroke has been accumulating for years, but was thought to have been given the definitive thumbs-up by the Antiplatelet Trialists' Collaboration (ATC) in a series of articles in 1994 (BMJ, 1994; 308: 81-106; 159-68; 235-46). These conclusions echoed many of the same group's discoveries six years earlier (BMJ, 1988; 296: 320-31). Even though those findings, on closer inspection, were more circumspect than many were willing to acknowledge at the time, aspirin quickly became hailed as the conquering hero of stroke treatment. It has since been prescribed widely (almost recklessly) throughout the world.

But the side effects of aspirin in the high doses which are prescribed for stroke treatment are debilitating and sometimes fatal. Aspirin is usually prescribed in doses ranging from 75 to 325 mg daily. Although this is lower than the megadoses of 1 to 4 g daily not uncommon 15 years ago, it is not without risk.

Dyspepsia (stomach upset, nausea and vomiting) and gastrointestinal haemorrhage can occur in 10 to 20 per cent of cases (Lancet, 31 May 1980). Even in low doses, it can actually increase the risk of cerebral haemorrhage. Although this rise is not statistically significant in high-risk patients, for the low-risk group the increase may be as high as 21 per cent (Drugs and Therapeutics Bulletin, 20 Jan 1994).

There is continuous debate over the optimum time that aspirin therapy should carry on (BMJ, 1994; 308: 71-3). Certainly, long-term use can cause serious side effects. Aspirin may slow blood clotting, but it can also deplete the body of certain essential vitamins and minerals, especially iron. Not surprisingly, one of the effects of long-term aspirin therapy is anaemia, a condition which can complicate haemorrhagic disorders. Other side effects include ulcers (particularly in elderly persons), liver damage and allergic reactions such as hives, wheezing, tinnitus, chronic catarrh, headache, confusion and, more rarely, hypotension followed by collapse. Asthmatics can die from severe attacks brought on by aspirin consumption. In combination with thrombolytics, such as warfarin or heparin, it may augment either the risks or the benefits of those agents, depending on which research one chooses to believe.

In addition, subsequent commentary on the ATC findings suggests that the researchers got it all wrong. Less than a year after the antiplatelet research was published, a small review appeared in the British Medical Journal questioning earlier findings (1994; 308: 1213-5). Researchers Alexander Cohen and his colleagues from the Thrombosis Research Institute took a closer look at the Collaboration's figures for the third arm of the trial, which examined at the effectiveness of aspirin in reducing venous thrombosis and pulmonary embolism in patients after surgery. They found not only that the researchers had compared trials which were not comparable, but also that some of the ATC arithmetic didn't add up.

The ATC study had also chosen to skirt the issue of substantial side effects, such as internal bleeding, because in many of the trials analysed these side effects were not recorded. But as Cohen and colleagues comment, "This information is not optional data for completeness but is absolutely essential to determine risk-benefit ratios, which must always be clearly defined before any general recommendations are made." These problems served to highlight several important issues, including the poor quality of research hitherto published in medical journals regarding stroke, its treatment and prevention, and the superficial, overly eager willingness of practitioners to latch on to any research, however inadequate, presented in an authoritative manner.

Not surprisingly, the authors of the ATC study defended their position in the same issue, declaring that their data was not intended as a recommendation for aspirin as a wholesale measure; that "treatment recommendations depend on a variety of considerations, of which trial results are only one part"; that it was up to individual physicians to familiarise themselves with all available data and the variety of treatments in current use; and that the best they could do was to rely on whatever research has been produced to date (BMJ, 1995; 309: 1215-7).

To some extent, they were justified. Aspirin cannot claim to prevent primary strokes and has never been proven effective as a preventatives in low-risk patients with no history of cardiovascular disorders (New Eng J Med, 1992; 327: 175-81; BMJ, 1988; 296: 313-6). Even as secondary prevention, for which there is some evidence, there is disagreement about the optimum dose (Lancet, 1991; 338: 1345-9). One trial comparing treatment with aspirin, warfarin or no treatment at all was revealing. In patients with a low risk of stroke, there was no significant difference in life expectancy between the three groups. In high-risk patients, life expectancy over the following 10-year period was 6.27 years for the aspirin group, 6.51 for warfarin users and 6.01 for those receiving no treatment at all—a statistically significant difference but close enough to provide food for thought (JAMA, 1995; 274: 1839-45).

With hindsight, the BMJ's response in the editorial which prefaced the ATC reports was telling: "Aspirin seems *as effective as* any other single agent or combination of agents [our emphasis]." (BMJ, 1994; 308: 71-3). In the end, that's not saying much since most other single agents or combination of agents produce devastating side effects, particularly in low- to medium-risk patients.

Since the ATC trial, the Cochrane Database of Systematic Reviews has published on disc the first set of overviews from the Cochrane Stroke Review Group. Among these, four trials of antiplatelet agents showed no significant advantage in rates for death, deep vein thrombosis or cerebral haemorrhage when compared to other methods of treatment (Stroke Module, Cochrane database of systematic reviews, Updated 9 March 1995).

Change your diet

Stroke prevention, like heart-disease prevention, is largely a matter of common sense. Lifestyle changes may be unlikely to produce immediate benefits; one study, for instance, concluded that dietary changes take about four years to significantly reduce blood pressure (JAMA, 22 May 1996). However, they are also unlikely to produce harmful or fatal side effects and may provide those with low to moderate risk of stroke with a better quality of life for longer.

A diet rich in fruit and vegetables can help protect against stroke. For every extra three servings (a serving is defined as half a cup) per day of fruit and vegetables you could reduce the risk of stroke by 22 per cent (JAMA, 1995; 273: 1113-7). Vegetables provide the greatest protection, perhaps because of their high fibre content (known to lower blood pressure). Fruit and vegetables contain a number of beneficial elements including carotenoids and vitamin C, as well as anti-nutrients, such as tannins, phytic acid, flavonoids, and phyto-oestrogens, all which have a cholesterol-lowering effect (BMJ, 1996; 312: 1479; 478-81; JAMA, 1995; 274: 1197).

The same substances can be found in things like red wine and tea, and moderate amounts of these may offer a protective effect. One Danish study of 6,051 men and 7,234 women aged 30 to 70 showed that those who had a moderate intake of red wine (three to five glasses a day) cut their risk of heart disease and stroke by half (BMJ,

6 May 1995). The flavonoids found in fruit, vegetables, wine and tea are potent antioxidants and have an antiplatelet effect (Biochem Pharmacol, 1987; 36: 317-22). Although platelet-inhibiting factors in flavonoids have a more direct effect on ischaemic stroke, they have also been shown to reduce the risk of haemorragic stroke (JAMA, 1995; 273: 317-22). The Danish study showed that abstainers had the highest risk, but the use of alcohol as a preventative needs to be weighed carefully against other debilitating side effects, such as depletion of minerals like magnesium, liver damage and, in some cases, cancer (New Eng J Med, 11 May 1995).

Eating walnuts has also been shown to help reduce the risk of stroke (JAMA, 1995, 273: 1563). Walnuts, along with soya bean or canola oil, provide a source of the essential fatty acid alpha-lineolic acid. Research shows that for every 0.13 per cent increase in alpha-lineolic acid in the blood, the risk of stroke drops 37 per cent. The reasons why are not fully understood, but it is thought that it may reduce the formation of blood clots that contribute to stroke.

Increase antioxidants

Stroke victims with a high level of vitamin A in the blood recover more quickly and are less likely to die than patients with lower levels (Lancet, 1992; 339: 1562-5). In fact, antioxidant vitamins such as A, C and E may help reduce the level of free radicals—the toxic by-products of metabolism. In elderly people in particular, higher levels of vitamin C can act as a protective agent against stroke (BMJ, 1995; 310: 1563-4).

Exercise

Aerobic exercise also cuts your risk of stroke. Starting regular exercise during adolescence has been found to significantly reduce the risk of suffering a stroke in later life. Researchers at Birmingham University's department of geriatric medicine found that vigorous exercise between the ages of 15 to 25 gave the most protection and that this was not affected by risk factors, such as social class, smoking, alcohol consumption, family history of stroke, hypertension or diet. Continued vigorous exercise later in life, especially up to the age of 55, also helped reduce the risk (BMJ, 1993; 307: 231-4). American research agrees: analysis of data from the 11-year national health and nutrition examination study showed clear evidence of the preventative benefits of exercise. In men and women with a sedentary lifestyle, the relative risk of stroke was almost double that of their active counterparts (Am J Epidemiology, 1996; 143: 860-9.)

Lose weight

Obesity can lead to hypertension. Analysis of one 36-year follow-up study suggests that one in four adults in the United States has hypertension and that 78 per cent of the hypertension in men and 65 per cent in women is directly related to obesity (New Eng J Med, 1996; 334: 1571-6).

Eat garlic

Garlic taken over a few months can reduce levels of cholesterol in the blood by 15 per cent and heart attack risk by 30 per cent. It also thins the blood, reducing the risk of thrombosis.

II

STANDARD MEDICAL TREATMENT

CHAPTER 4

DRUGS THERAPY

Half of all heart attack victims die after their first attack. The other half, more often than not, wander the earth in an imitation of life, popping pills and practising self denial. Heart attacks are scary, and the average victim doesn't want a repeat. On this basis, many feel grateful for the bewildering array of treatments—vasodilators, antiarrhythmics, antihypertensives, diuretics, cholesterol drugs and surgical techniques—which are on offer. Some invest these things with magic, life-giving potential, though there is little evidence in many instances that they do any good at all.

While early mortality from heart attacks—death within the first 15 days to a year, depending on which study you read—appears to be on the decline, the incidence of heart failure is increasing (Lancet, 1993; 341: 733-6). In the US, about 1 per cent of the population is having a heart attack at any one time (Cardiol Clin, 1989; 7: 1-9). In the UK, about 1 million patients per year currently receive treatment for heart attacks. The question is, is it doing any good?

One long-term trial in Finland showed that patients on the receiving end of multiple interventions were actually more likely to die from heart failure than those who received no interventions (JAMA, 1991; 266: 1225-9). Another trial in Gottenburg which followed 10,000 middle-aged men for 10 years showed no reduction in mortality from a multiple intervention programme (Eur Heart J,

1986; 7: 279-88). Another trial of more than 12,000 men showed similar results (JAMA, 1982; 248: 1465-77; JAMA, 1990; 263: 1795-801), as did a WHO study of 61,000 men (Lancet, 1986; i: 869-72). In fact, in the British arm of the WHO study, the death rate from heart disease was 8 per cent higher in the intervention group (Lancet, 1983; i: 1062-6).

Indeed, the latest study from North America demonstrates that this get-in-there-early, aggressive intervention doesn't do one bit of good. The study, which compared the use of cardiac procedures and mortality rates of more than a quarter of a million elderly patients in both Canada and the US, found that America had strikingly higher rates of aggressive cardiac treatment than Canada: 11 times the rate of angioplasty and 10 times the rate of bypass surgery. Although short-term mortality after a heart attack was slightly lower in the US initially (21 versus 22 per cent), this small difference disappeared after a year. In the long-term, survival rates were virtually identical between the two countries (New Eng J Med, 1997; 336: 1500-5).

Drug treatment doesn't seem to provide long-term gains. A single drug can act in several different ways, sometimes unpredictably. Trials have shown that combining drugs can be fatal. For example, in trials where enalapril (an ACE inhibitor) or hydralazine (a vasodilator/antihypertensive) and isosorbide dinitrate (also a vasodilator) when added to digoxin (a glycoside to increase the force of the heart beat) and used in combination with diuretics (to treat hypertension), survival rates did improve during the trial—but not by much. Nevertheless, within four years more than 40 per cent of the patients enrolled in these trials were dead (N Eng J Med, 1987; 316: 1429-35; N Eng J Med, 1991; 325: 293-302; N Eng J Med, 1991; 325: 303-10; N Eng J Med, 1986; 314: 1547-52). Other studies show between a 3 and 7 per cent short-term (30-35 days) post-heart attack survival rate with early drug treatment (Lancet, 1994; 343: 311-22; N Eng J Med, 1993; 329: 673-82). While these numbers may provide comfort for the few who survive, they call into question the real benefit of conventional treatments as well as the policy of concentrating merely on keeping patients alive, rather than encouraging them to take steps to improve the quality of their lives.

Heart attack, or myocardial infarction ("death" of the heart muscle—caused by an inadequate blood supply) is often caused by obstruction of the coronary artery due to atherosclerosis. The condition may occur suddenly or after a history of angina pectoris (chest pains). Some people have little evidence of blockage, in which case it is assumed that spasm of the coronary artery is responsible. To treat these two possible causes, patients are offered a range of drugs to unclog and/or dilate arteries, to thin the blood or strengthen the force of the heart beat.

Beta-blockers—which have an anti-arrhythmic as well as an antihypertensive action—only reduce the possibility of a further heart attack by a very small margin and have other implications for a person's health. They cause dizziness, impotence, nausea, coldness in the extremities, nightmares and insomnia.

Beta-blockers can also produce sudden, irregular heart beats which can cause death. One trial was stopped early because the side effects were so alarming (Lancet, 1996; 348: 7-12), and the editorial which accompanied this research concluded that we must assume that all anti-arrhythmic drugs are potentially lethal.

Calcium-channel blockers can stop blood coagulating, but what is good for the heart is not necessarily good for the stomach. They have been shown to cause severe stomach bleeding in the elderly (Lancet, 1996; 347: 1056). They can also double your risk of getting cancer (Lancet, 1996; 348: 49).

Anti-arrhythmics can cause the problem they are trying to treat. In one large trial, there were significant deaths in those taking encainide and flecainide. Nearly 6 per cent of patients died from arrhythmias (abnormal heart rhythms) while taking these drugs, as opposed to 2.2 per cent of those who took placebo (N Eng J Med, 1991; 324: 781-8). Equally, nearly 3 per cent died of heart attack, compared with 0.7 per cent of the placebo group.

In the three-year SOLVD (Studies of Left Ventricular Dysfunction) trial, ACE inhibitors prevented three episodes of non-fatal heart failure for each 100 patients treated per year. Because of this, it has been suggested that patients should be given ACE inhibitors to prevent further episodes (N Eng J Med, 1992; 327: 725-7). But a look at the long-term picture is revealing: ACE inhibitors (in this case enalapril) saved only one life for every 300 patients treated (N Eng J Med, 1992; 327: 685-91).

One of the most commonly prescribed drugs for the treatment of heart failure is digitalis (digoxin), even though its long-term benefits and safety have never been proven. The Digitalis Investigation Group thought that, after 200 years of usage, it was about time a proper study on the drug was conducted. They gave 3,397 heart patients 0.25 mg a day of digoxin and another 3,403 patients a placebo, plus diuretics and ACE inhibitors, for three years. At the end of the study period, just as many patients on the drug died as those given the placebo. The one crumb of comfort for the pro-digitalis brigade was that those on the drug needed 6 per cent fewer hospitalisations (New Eng J Med, 1997; 336: 525-33).

Another route gaining credence in traditional medicine is thrombolysis therapy, using drugs to clear blockages. Nevertheless, research reveals a high failure rate. A study in Northern Ireland tested two of the drugs—Kabikinase and Eminase—on 37 patients in a 129-strong patient group. The 37 received early therapy—as soon as the symptoms of heart trouble were diagnosed, while the remainder were given the treatment only on admission to hospital.

Within 14 days, one patient on early treatment had died against 10 in the second group; after one year, two had died in the early-treatment group against 17 in the second. At the end of the two-year trial, another four had died in the second group only.

Researchers have found that thrombolysis is actually just as effective as angioplasty in preventing death in patients who suffer from serious heart problems. The latest research compared 1,050 patients given angioplasty with 2,095 treated with thrombolysis who were admitted to hospitals in Seattle, Washington. Risk of death was 5.6 per cent in the thrombolysis patients, and 5.5 per cent among those given angioplasty (N Engl J Med, 1996; 335: 1253-60).

Clearly, drugs therapy is the least traumatic and least expensive of the treatments. But while the Northern Irish study was testing the effectiveness of the treatment on diagnosis, it also showed that the mortality rate by using the drugs was nearly 15 per cent—an uncomfortably high figure.

Combination heart drugs

Most doctors think that if one drug does some good, then two will double the benefits. The beta-blocker/calcium-channel blocker combination has become very popular for patients with coronary artery disease. The thinking behind this is that a low dose of both drugs will decrease the number and severity of attacks of angina more effectively than a high dose of one of the drugs alone, and with fewer side effects.

Since many factors influence the balance between the supply of oxygen to the heart and its demands, and a single drug can only counter a few of these factors, doctors have simply assumed that a second heart drug with different chemical actions might work in a complementary fashion. Because drugs for angina often cause rebound circulatory effects, which work against their effectiveness, the other assumption has been that these unwanted effects can be counteracted by a second drug.

However, these two assumptions have never stood up to scientific scrutiny. According to one review of a number of controlled clinical trials, combining a calcium-channel blocker with a low-dose beta-blocker rarely has any additional benefits for angina patients, and can actually increase adverse reactions by up to 60 per cent (New Eng J Med, 1989; 320: 709-18).

The other problem is that most doctors don't really understand how each of these drugs relieves angina on its own. Beta-blockers work by blocking the receptors in the heart from receiving impulses from chemicals released during effort or stress. This action inhibits the rise in heart rate and blood pressure during exertion, so it has always been assumed that the drugs relieve angina and other symptoms of coronary artery disease by decreasing heart-oxygen demand. Because electrical impulses from the heart (which control the contraction and relaxation that occur with every beat) are channelled through calcium ions, calcium-channel blockers—which work by slowing down these electrical instructions—theoretically slow down your heartbeat. They also help to dilate arteries, increasing the flow of blood and supposedly easing the work the heart has to do to pump blood through the body. Consequently, many doctors have operated on the assumption that calcium-channel blockers relieve areas in the body with blocked blood vessels by increasing the supply of oxygen to the heart. This notion—that beta-blockers and calcium-channel blockers somehow work in tandem by increasing heart oxygen supply and lowering demand—is behind the strong support among the medical community for their combined use. However, both drugs actually alleviate angina through strikingly similar effects—including reducing the heart's oxygen consumption, limiting the rise in heart rate, redistributing the blood flow from the heart and relaxing the blood vessels.

In fact, recent observations show that the two drugs don't necessarily interact well together. Although calcium-channel blockers can stop the arterial constriction in the heart caused by beta-blockers, this may only occur in areas of the body with normal blood flow, and they may only further reduce blood flow in those areas of the heart already under threat. By the same token, while beta-blockers may prevent the rapid heart rate induced by calcium-channel blockers, this may do nothing to prevent the lowered blood pressure calcium-channel blockers frequently cause. Calcium blockers may even worsen angina if blood pressure falls markedly.

In many other ways, the two operate antagonistically. Beta-blockers can increase the lowering effect on blood pressure of the calcium-channel blockers, and so increase the risk of poor blood supply to the heart. The combination can also exacerbate angina if the two drugs combine to cause rapid heartbeat. Beta-blockers can also cancel out the ability of calcium-channel blockers to relax the blood vessels. Abnormally low blood pressure, causing dizziness and sudden falls, worsening heart failure and conduction defects (that is, problems with electrical instructions from the brain) may occur more often during combination therapy than with single drug therapy (New Eng J Med, 1989; 320: 709-18).

"Numerous case reports have documented the occurrence of hypotension, bradycardias [abnormally slow heartbeat] and worsening heart failure when each of the three calcium-entry blocking drugs has been used in combination with beta-blockers," says the author of the study. They also depress the ability of the heart to contract.

The author also warns that of all the calcium-channel blocking drugs, verapamil (which sells as brand names Cordilox, Berkatens, Securon, Isoptin and Univer) is the most likely to interact unfavourably with beta-blockers. Besides inhibiting the heart's ability to contract, the combined therapy could dangerously impair the ability of your sympathetic nervous system to keep your circulatory system in equilibrium. It could also enhance the effect of beta-blockers. This combination may also slow the elimination of the drugs from your body, thus enhancing their adverse effects.

Heart drugs: dangers at a glance

Vasodilators (nitrates, calcium-channel blockers):
Headaches; dizziness; hypotension; and potentially fatal altered heart rhythm (either too fast or too slow). Calcium-channel blockers can

cause constipation; vomiting; oedema; sudden rapid heart beats; liver disorders; rashes; depression and gastrointestinal disorders.

Antihypertensives (ACE inhibitors, diruetics, potassium-channel blockers):
• ACE inhibitors can cause sudden drops in the blood pressure, a dangerous rise in potassium levels and, when used with some diuretics, fluid on the lungs. Also, kidney malfunction; muscle cramps; diarrhea; nausea; fatigue; rashes; abdominal pain; heart palpitations; jaundice; sleep disturbances; mood swings; and impotence.
• Diuretics can cause gastrointestinal disturbances; dry mouth; skin rashes; photosensitivity; kidney damage; and pancreatitis.

Beta-blockers:
Potentially fatal slowing of the heart; asthma; fatigue; cold hands and feet; sleep disturbances; nightmares; stomach upsets, and rashes.

Anti-arrhythmics:
Heart failure; chest pain; choking sensations; light-headedness; impaired vision; skin discolouration; phototoxicity; diarrhoea; fever; lupus-like symptoms; psychosis; and liver damage.

Antiplatelets (aspirin, anticoagulants):
Gastrointestinal problems; respiratory disorders; stroke; diarrhoea; vomiting; throbbing headaches; and hypotension.

Cholesterol-lowering drugs:
Severe depression; suicidal violent tendencies; constipation; vitamin K deficiency; and impotence. Also an established link with cancer of the lung, thyroid, testis and lymph nodes.

CHAPTER 5
SURGERY AND OTHER MODERN MEDICAL PROCEDURES

If your doctor suspects that something is awry, he may trot you off for angiography, an x-ray of the heart with a contrast dye to examine the state of your arteries. But there is plenty of evidence that this test has a pretty poor batting average, wrongfully setting in motion one of a number of potentially lethal heart operations.

In one test in Boston, half of the 171 patients who had earlier been recommended to have a coronary angioplasty on the basis of their angiograph were found to not need the operation. In the end, only 4 per cent of the patients advised to have an angiograph really needed one (JAMA, 1992; 268: 2537-40).

Angiographs are also especially open to misinterpretation. In another study in which the pathology reports of deceased patients were compared with prior angiographs, two-thirds were found to be wrong (Circulation, 1981; 63: 24; 27).

Angioplasty

If you are one of the lucky minority to be diagnosed with a heart condition before suffering a fatal attack—usually because of severe pains, breathlessness or difficulty in walking—the chances are that your doctor will recommend angioplasty.

Coronary balloon angioplasty—or percutaneous transluminal coronary angioplasty (PTCA), to give its proper name—has been touted as the miracle preventative for heart attacks and the major method of treating heart problems.

Angioplasty has been in the ascendant since it was first mentioned in The Lancet in 1978. It is a relatively simple procedure which involves the threading of a tiny balloon through blocked arteries and expanding it to clear them, usually by pressing atheronatous (fatty) plaques against the coronary artery wall.

When angioplasty started to be used, the "gee-whizz" technique at the time was coronary bypass surgery, then one of the wonders of the modern medical world.

As angioplasty became more sophisticated, so it gained ground on bypass surgery, which "bypasses" blockages by creating new pathways using genuine arteries from the patient or synthetic tubing. Angioplasty was considered cheaper, easier to perform and far less traumatic, and is now seen virtually as the heart disease cure-all, offered to angina sufferers, those recovering from a heart attack, and as a just-in-case remedy for those concerned about the state of their arteries.

In 1990, 200,000 people in the US were treated with the procedure, and a further 100,000 in Europe, yet "only a few prospective trials had assessed its efficacy", stated the New England Journal of Medicine (1992; 326: 57-8).

Not that the medical profession had much to worry about, it seemed. Initial tests showed an extraordinary success rate, some ranging above 90 per cent, with complications in fewer than 10 per cent of cases. Even Mother Teresa, in her 81st year, received the treatment, giving it a by then unneeded added endorsement.

One of the most comprehensive surveys to date vindicated the results. Of 5,827 patients treated with angioplasty between January and June 1991 in New York, 88 per cent were reported as being successful (JAMA, 1992; 268: 3092-7). However, as the researchers wrote at the end of the report, "no data on postdischarge complications are available"—a throwaway line that calls into question the real long-term effectiveness of the treatment.

Ironically, it was The Lancet, the journal that had first announced the new wonder treatment, that was in the vanguard of those voicing concerns. A delegate from the journal attended an angioplasty course in 1991 and wrote that he "tended to take a less favourable view of the outcome than the clinician doing the procedure, and in general the results of coronary angioplasty seemed inferior to those reported in journals" (Lancet, 1992; 340: 1202-5).

In the US, an even more damning statement was issued by the American College of Cardiologists: "Observations raise the question of whether cardiology has focused too much on doing coronary angioplasty procedures rather than on addressing who needs it, what are the criteria, and what are the results. Is angioplasty being done for cardiologists or for patients?" This represented a remarkable *volte face* by a profession normally protective of its procedures.

Far from being an instant miracle cure-all, the truth about angioplasty is much more complicated:

• Angioplasty is no better than drug therapy in preventing death (N Eng J Med, 1996; 335; 1253-60).

• It is more effective for simple cases. A study in Boston, Massachusetts, discovered that angioplasty patients with two to three risk factors had a survival rate over five years of just 13 per cent (New Eng J Med, 1992; 327: 1329-35).

• Stenosis (narrowing of the artery) recurs within six months after angioplasty—with the diameter of the blood vessel being only 16 per cent larger than before treatment, according to the American College of Cardiologists. In one Italian study, restenosis occurred in 73 per cent of cases (New Eng J Med, 1991; 326: 1053-7).

• Because of the need for continual re-treatment and monitoring, the real costs of angioplasty may be much higher than those for drug therapy in cases of mild angina and single-vessel disease. A study in Maryland estimated that hospital charges had doubled in the 10 years that angioplasty has been used (New Eng J Med, 1992; 326: 10-16).

• The effectiveness of the treatment in triple-vessel disease (when two-thirds of each artery is blocked) was further questioned by an Italian study, which reported only a 52 per cent success rate in those cases. It was also successful in only 30 per cent of cases of total blockage of the artery (Chest, 1992; 102: 375-9).

• It has a very low success rate with blocked arteries in the lower part of the body. If those type of blockages aren't treated, the patient can end up having a leg amputated. Despite an increase in the use of the treatment for lower-body blockages from one per 100,000 to 24 per 100,000, between 1979 and 1989 in Maryland, the number of leg amputations remained constant, at 30 per 100,000 (New Eng J Med, 1991; 325: 556-62).

• There is also strong evidence that many of the angioplasty operations carried out may be unnecessary. A damning American study looked at 171 patients who had earlier been referred for angioplasty, and concluded that for half of them the operation either wasn't needed or could be safely deferred (JAMA, 1992; 268: 2537-40). They also pointed out that coronary angioplasty was originally expected to replace bypass surgery, but in fact, both techniques have grown in tandem, with neither reducing the frequency of the other. "Evident over the past decade is the ever lowering threshold for carrying out bypass as well as angioplasty . . . even asymptomatic patients are not exempt," they say.

Atherectomy

Atherectomy is a technique for unclogging blocked heart vessels, which is meant to be an improvement over angioplasty by solving the thorny problem of restenosis. Nevertheless, so far it compares poorly with the technique it was intended to replace.

In a study of 1000 patients (New Eng J Med, 1993; 329: 221-7), the heart vessels of those having atherectomy were less blocked after treatment than those having angioplasty. Yet this apparent success is undermined by the fact that "the probability of death [or heart attack] within six months was higher in the atherectomy group (8.6 per cent vs 4.6 per cent)," according to the authors of the study. Two other important trials showed little or no difference between the two techniques in terms of the subsequent rate of reclogging arteries (New Eng J Med, 1993; 329: 221-7).

Stents

Given the high rate of failure of balloon angioplasty, it was only a matter of time before someone came up with a new, better gadget to combat stubbornly clogged arteries.

The result was the stent—a tiny, stainless steel coil used to shore up collapsed or clogged arteries. Stenting has become increasingly popular with cardivascular surgeons. In the US, in 1998, more than 500,000 patients were referred to stent surgeries. The procedure is also becoming more common among European surgeons.

The stent is shunted into the artery over a balloon-covered catheter. Once in place, the balloon is inflated to expand the diameter of the coil. In theory, it should keep the artery open, improving blood flow to the heart. But several problems have been noted with the stent. Although it opens the artery more than angioplasty does, it is also associated with a high rate of restenosis—the arteries narrowing again.

Stented patients also run a higher risk of subacute thrombosis. This is because blood clots form around any foreign object in the body. To avert this, patients with stents are often put on anti-coagulant drugs such as aspirin, warfarin and ticlopidine for months after the stent is inserted (N Eng J Med, 1998, 339: 1672-78).

To get around the clotting problem, there has been continued experimentation with stents coated with anti-coagulants, stents coated with human tissue and even stents covered with polyester sleeves, mostly to no avail. However, in the rush to build a better stent, doctors seem to have ignored some of the disturbing evidence about their effects.

While there is some evidence that combining angioplasty with stenting may make a positive difference in the short term (J Am Col Cardiol 1998; 31: 23-30), long-term research into their use is thin on the ground. Equally, while stents may prove effective for those with congenital heart defects, there is still little evidence that they are widely appropriate for those suffering from heart disease due to lifestyle factors.

What is known is that certain patients do worse on them. Insulin-dependent diabetics who have stents implanted in their coronary arteries following balloon angioplasty are more likely to develop complications and die in the year after the procedure than non-diabetics (J Am Coll Cardiol, 1998; 32: 584-9). This effect was not noted, however, in non-insulin dependent diabetics.

Elderly patients also experience more problems after stenting. The risk of complications, "heart events" and death is greatest in the first month after the procedure (J Am Coll Cardiol, 1998; 32: 577-83).

It seems the best we can say about stents at the moment is that for a small group of heart sufferers (those with congenital malformations or those undergoing a heart transplant) they may provide some benefit. For the majority, however, stents don't cure heart disease, they merely postpone it.

Bypass surgery

Although angioplasty is fast becoming the operation of choice for those with a heart condition, it seems to be less effective than the bypass surgery it is superseding.

A study by the University Hospital in Nottingham indicated that bypass surgery may be more successful at treating angina than angioplasty. A survey of 1,011 patients showed that six times as many angioplasty patients needed repeat treatment or surgery as those who had bypass surgery. The report also found that angina was almost three times as common in angioplasty patients as in bypass patients within six months of the treatment (Lancet, 1993; 341: 573-80; 599-600).

Even more recent research, which examined more than 1000 patients from 26 heart centres around Europe, shows that the survival rate among patients in the first year after angioplasty is lower than among those who have major bypass surgery. Angioplasty patients also need to be on more medication than those given a bypass, and are more likely to need a repeat operation within the first year (New Eng J Med, 1994; 331: 1037-43; Lancet, 1995; 346: 1179-84).

In another study, angioplasty patients were able to return to work earlier, but bypass patients could perform more daily activities, such as housework and walking. Both procedures added an average of 4.4 years to the lives of patients. But 26 per cent of the patients suffered from angina after the first year in the angioplasty group, compared to 11 per cent of the bypass patients. Nearly 60 per cent of the angioplasty group had to have further treatment because their arteries started to clog up again (N Eng J Med, 1997; 336: 92-9).

Two clinical trials have concluded that neither one of the two procedures has been shown to make a substantial difference in terms of saving lives, preventing heart attacks or increasing arterial blood flow after three years. One of these studies, carried out by Spencer King and his colleagues from the Emory University School of Medicine in Atlanta, Georgia, concludes that the choice can be left to the patient and the quality of life he wants afterwards (New Eng J Med, 1994; 331: 1044-9).

In a peer review of this research, David Hillis and John Rutherford at the Southwestern Medical Center in Dallas, Texas, point out that surgery is not even necessary if the patient has normal functioning of the left side of the heart. "Lest we forget, medical therapy relieves angina in many patients regardless of the severity of disease, and its influence on survival is similar to that of surgery," they write in the same issue of the journal.

The two studies discovered that only half of the patients who took part—5,118 in one, and 8,981 patients in the other study—were suitable for angioplasty. Both studies agreed that bypass is a more dangerous procedure, with a greater risk of a fatal heart attack on the operating table, but those patients who survive it can enjoy a longer period without further medication. The angioplasty patient, however, needs to go on a course of drugs and may need a repeat operation.

It's not all good news for bypass surgery, which has been associated with a high rate of stroke following the procedure. About 6 per cent of patients may suffer a stroke directly afterwards. Of these, 5 per cent die and nearly half suffer deterioration in mental functions (N Eng J Med, 1996; 335: 1857-63).

In the 1970s, several major studies revealed that bypass surgery did not improve survival except among patients with severe coronary disease, particularly to the left ventricle. It did, however, relieve severe angina (New Eng J Med, 1992; 326: 56-8).

However, bypass surgery is most appropriate in treating those with triple-vessel disease. This covers just 10 per cent of all heart-condition sufferers. Bypass surgery is, of course, a major and traumatic procedure, and the death rate has ranged from as low as 3 per cent to an alarming 23 per cent in the US.

Even though it is an appropriate treatment for just such a small percentage of sufferers, the bypass seems to be surviving better than its patients. Perhaps this is not surprising when you consider that in the US, it is one of the best-paying surgical procedures, with surgeons earning about $50,000 an operation. Overall, the treatment costs Americans $5 billion a year, to treat just 200,000 people.

So what should you do if you are diagnosed as at risk from heart disease? Despite the impression given by many doctors, heart surgery is often not urgent. Dr Wayne Perry—a proponent of chelation therapy as an alternative to surgery (see p 96)—suggests patients should discuss with their doctor the possibility of deferring a heart operation for a year while they try other, less invasive methods of treatment, such as changes to diet, exercise and stress-management programmes, possibly combined with chelation therapy. Only if these other methods don't work should you think about going ahead with surgery.

III

ALTERNATIVE TREATMENT

CHAPTER 6

THE NEW HEART DIETS

Over the years, many experts have promoted many different diets for a healthy heart. Among the most famous is the very low-fat regime promoted by doctors like Nathan Pritikin and Dean Ornish.

Although Dean Ornish is considered by many to be the guru of heart, he is following a trail blazed by the late Nathan Pritikin, who was a scientist, inventor and founder of the Pritikin Center in Santa Monica, California. Originally, he devised a new way of eating—which involved drastically cutting down on fats and salt, reducing intake of animal proteins and sugar, and increasing consumption of complex carbohydrates—in order to cure his own heart problems. He then turned his experience of improving health into an eating system. His plan became a bestseller with a good track record for reversing atherosclerosis, diabetes, constipation and other modern health problems. The Pritikin plan advised patients to eat:

- whole grains
- vegetables—fresh, canned or frozen (except avocados and olives)
- fruit—fresh, cooked, canned or frozen (except coconut) and small amounts of unsweetened dried fruit—limited because of its high sugar content

- an average of three ounces daily of lean, meat, skinless chicken and fish
- one glass of skim milk and two ounces of non-fat green Sapsago cheese or cottage cheese daily
- linden tea
- egg whites if desired.

Exercise is also an important part of the Pritikin programme. In addition, the diet forbids all fats, oils, avocados, olives, salty meats, full fat dairy products, soya beans and table salt. It also doesn't allow for foods containing refined carbohydrates, such as sugar, honey, molasses, fructose, bleached white flour, white rice and pasta—except in very limited amounts—as well as caffeinated drinks, whole eggs and egg yolks, alcoholic beverages and soft drinks.

About 10 per cent of calories on the Pritikin plan are obtained from fats, 10 to 12 per cent from proteins and 80 per cent from complex carbohydrates.

The Pritikin diet is less popular today, though in one study it still showed good results in slowing the progression of heart disease (Am J Cardiol, 1997; 79: 1112-4). In its day, it certainly represented a radical departure from the standard Western diet. But it lacked the media-friendly appeal of his predecessor Dean Ornish—or maybe all that was missing was access to the Internet.

Dean Ornish is the president of the Preventive Medicine Research Institute in Sausalito, California. He is passionate in his belief that a very low fat, vegetarian diet is the only way forward for those suffering from heart disease. To prove his point, he has followed over the years a small and ever dwindling group of subjects—many with severe heart disease—who have followed his strict regime. His studies on this group have been used—mostly by him—as conclusive proof that his approach works.

Ornish's treatment plan includes a vegetarian diet with less than

10 per cent of calories from fat—a significantly lower level than the 30 per cent widely recommended by heart associations and the WHO. In his diet, saturated fat is kept to an absolute minimum. Although we tend to focus on Ornish's dietary recommendations as central (perhaps because they are easiest to measure through medical research), he himself believes that each facet of the programme—moderate exercise, stress management techniques, including breathing, yoga and meditation, group support/ counselling sessions, stopping smoking and no use of lipid-lowering drugs—is equally important.

Ornish's reversal diet is very strict. In summary, it:

- has almost no cholesterol
- has less than 10 per cent of calories from fat, little of it saturated
- excludes foods high in saturated fats, such as avocados, nuts and seeds
- is high in fibre
- allows but does not encourage alcohol (less than 2 ounces per day)
- excludes all oils and all animal products except non-fat milk and yoghurt
- allows egg whites
- excludes caffeine and other stimulants, such as MSG
- allows moderate use of sugar and salt
- is not restricted in calories.

Over the years, he has conducted a series of very small studies on the same group of 28 people to see if a comprehensive programme of intensive lifestyle changes can have a positive impact on the progression of coronary heart disease. To be fair, Ornish's results with his subjects do appear impressive. But in reality, they raise more questions than they answer. In Dr Ornish's first study (Lancet, 1990; 336: 129-33), known as the Lifestyle Heart Trial, he followed a group of 48 individuals who were randomly assigned either to take part in Ornish's regime or to be placed in a usual care group.

While the experimental group followed Ornish's plan, the control group followed a more conventional dietary treatment, averaging up to 30 per cent of their calories from fat and 200 mg cholesterol per day.

The main finding of the study was that 91 per cent in the Ornish group reported a decrease in angina attacks, as opposed to the other group, which experienced a 165 per cent increase. This seems impressive, but pertinent information seems to be missing.

Significantly, the usual care group did not receive a prescribed exercise programme, group support, counselling, instruction in stress management or smoking cessation. What, in fact, constituted "usual care" was not disclosed. The authors simply commented that this group "were not asked to make lifestyle changes, though they were free to do so". By this definition, "usual care" could be interpreted as having little or no care at all; and the conclusions of the study would be that making comprehensive lifestyle changes is a lot better than doing nothing at all. It's not a conclusion that you could argue with, but neither is it an astounding piece of research.

A few years later, Dr Ornish reported in the American Journal of Cardiology (1992; 69: 845-53) on the progress of the same patients after four years. By this time, eight patients had dropped out of the study, taken medication or had surgery, which disqualified them, or died—we are not told which—six in the experimental group and two in the control group. The 22 patients who continued to follow the experimental programme for four years on average showed less blockage in their arteries and improved blood flow to their hearts. The 18 patients in the usual care group showed more blockages in their arteries and less blood flow to their hearts after four years than after one year.

Again it looks promising, but there continued to be flaws. Clearly, from the beginning, the two groups were not comparable. Ornish, in this study and others which have been published since, has been reluctant to describe fully what constituted conventional or "usual care" in his studies, although it was later thought to be loosely modelled on the AHA Step I plan (see p 81). Usual care may mean prescribing often ineffective antihypertensive or cholesterol-lowering drugs (see chapters 1 and 2). However, patients in this study were selected on the basis that they were not taking drugs, at least initially. We are not told how many were prescribed drugs during the course of the studies.

Also, when considering Ornish's conclusions it is worth remembering that this study group consisted of people who often had quite advanced heart disease. The effectiveness of the plan may be simply that it is an emergency intervention for lifestyles that were already quite self-destructive. Whichever way you look at it, a study group of 48 people is simply too small to draw firm conclusions from. And although blockages did improve, the patients in Ornish's group still had heart disease and remained at risk. A significant number, given the small study size, had heart episodes which included bypass surgery, angioplasty and nonfatal heart attacks.

But perhaps the biggest unanswered question is what toll such a strict and time-consuming regime takes on the lives of those involved and on their families. It requires great effort to stay on it, as the dwindling numbers in Ornish's study suggest, and may even have a negative impact on their day-to-day quality of life. This, of course, is speculation since these ideas have not been addressed through study. Nevertheless they are important considerations.

The American Heart Association Diet

In contrast to Ornish, the AHA's plan for heart health is much more general and considered by many to be more "do-able" for the average person. The Association's guidelines, which are reflected in the guidelines of other medical organisations, such as the British Heart Association, include:

- eating a variety of foods
- reducing fat consumption, especially saturated fat and cholesterol
- losing weight
- increasing complex carbohydrates and dietary fibre
- reducing sodium intake
- consuming alcohol in moderation
- increasing physical activity
- quitting smoking

For those who have already suffered angina pains or other symptoms suggestive of heart and circulatory problems, the AHA spells it out more clearly in their Step I and Step II diet plans. Step I is an initial therapy for those who have not reduced their fat and cholesterol intake prior to conventional treatment. In it, patients are advised to limit their total fat to around 30 per cent or less of the day's calories from fat (thus, on a 3000-calorie-a-day diet, an individual would take in the higher level of 100 mg daily of fat, while on a 1500-calorie-a-day diet, the intake would be 50 mg daily). Of these, 8 to 10 per cent should come from saturated fatty acids, 10 per cent from polyunsaturated acids and up to 15 per cent from monounsaturated fatty acids.

The AHA diet also recommends consumption of less than 300 mg daily of cholesterol and no more than 2.4 g of sodium. Complex carbohydrates should make up approximately 55 to 60 per cent of your total calories.

The Step II diet, recommended for those whose cholesterol levels are in the high-risk range or who have had a heart attack, is a little more restrictive: 7 per cent or less saturated fatty acids and less than 200 mg daily of cholesterol.

In fairness, the AHA diet, while founded on some research evidence, has not been subject to rigorous testing, either. It is clearly easier for the majority of people to follow than Ornish's diet, and it may be more than adequate for those who are at a low to moderate risk of heart disease.

Making Comparisons

Not long after his second study, Ornish and his colleagues published a study which examined the heart health of his group and those on an dietary plan similar to that of the AHA Step I (JAMA, 1995; 274: 894-901). He used positron emission tomography to examine the health of the participants' arteries. The study group continued to dwindle, now containing 20 of his patients and 15 who were receiving usual care. But once again the Ornish regime showed a moderate reversal of heart disease among 99 per cent of his patients, while those in the standard care group showed a worsening of the disease.

Ornish tried again to compare his regime with that of the AHA. In his most recent study, he suggests that the combination of a very low-fat diet and yoga (and other stress-reduction techniques) can dramatically reverse heart disease (JAMA, 1998; 280: 2001-7). This study looked at 20 of his original experimental patients and 15 control patients who were following the AHA's Step II diet. As before, the patients were all part of the original Lifestyle Heart Trial.

Researchers at Ornish's institute and those from the University of California at San Francisco found that over the five years there was a reported 72 per cent reduction in the number of attacks of angina or chest pain in the experimental group, while those on the AHA diet experienced only a 36 per cent decrease. Cholesterol was also lower in Ornish's group, even though there were many AHA patients taking cholesterol-lowering drugs. The study cites a nearly 8 per cent improvement in the condition of their arteries, compared with the AHA patients, who experienced an 11 per cent increase in artery blockage.

Ornish believed that the study, five years on from his initial study, finally answered the most common criticism of his regime— namely that it was too strict for most people to follow. This seems an optimistic spin on things since only 20 of the original 28 completed the full five years.

During the trial, two patients in the experimental group suffered heart deaths and two others nonfatal heart attacks. In addition, there were two bypass surgeries and eight angioplasties. To be fair, although there was only one heart death in the conventional care group, there were four nonfatal heart attacks, five bypass surgeries and 14 angioplasties. It seems that neither group can claim complete success.

Comparing the two regimes may be a pointless exercise since Ornish's plan is geared toward reversing the progression of heart disease. Other researchers have found similarly good results with diet modifications (JAMA, 1960; 173: 884-8; J Fam Pract, 1995; 41: 560-8), although some of these allowed the use of cholesterol-lowering drugs. The AHA Step I plan, however, is a preventive one, recommended to help healthy individuals or those with mild to moderate risk, to prevent a worsening of their conditions. Indeed, Ornish's plan shows the most remarkable results on those who are at the highest risk.

Ornish's regime is unlikely to be an appropriate diet for everyone. It is certainly not recommended for pregnant women, the very elderly, those with diabetes or who are in any other way immune compromised. It may also hold risks for some due to its high carbohydrate intake. High carbohydrate typically increases blood fat (triglyceride) levels and lowers HDL cholesterol. Those with hypertriglyceridemia need to be monitored very closely if following the regime. In some people, reduced-fat, high-carbohydrate diets result in adverse metabolic changes, including reducing HDL cholesterol and increasing triglyceride levels (JAMA, 1995; 274: 1450-5).

What is highly likely is that preventing heart disease doesn't require the same strictness as reversing it—another good reason for not waiting until your body breaks down before making dietary and lifestyle changes.

Very low fat diets—what the research says

There is no question that lowering saturated fat combined with weight loss offers an effective strategy for lowering the risk of cardiovascular disease.

However, what constitutes "optimum" levels of fat and cholesterol are open to wide interpretation. One of the biggest criticisms of the Ornish regime is that it lowers fat at the expense of other important dietary factors such as essential nutrients like EFAs.

It must be stressed that studies of both Ornish and Pritikin regimes involved very small numbers and follow-up is limited. Questions about long-term adequacy of nutrients remain unanswered, and the belief that such regimes should be recommended to a wide population simply cannot be supported. Nevertheless, a wide body of official and unofficial support exists, particularly for Ornish's regime. On the Internet, for example, many health sites unquestioningly promote his low-fat regime as a scientifically proven miracle worker. We have looked at many of the elements which are part of Ornish's regime elsewhere in this book. There seems little doubt that meditation, stress reduction, emotional support all have a valid role to play in maintaining heart health. But what of the diet's very low fat content and strict adherence to a vegetarian regime? Are these the reasons why Ornish's plan appears to work so well?

Only the World Health Organisation study group's recommendations for fat intake come anywhere close to the lower level recommended in Ornish's regime. The WHO recommends that fat intake should be around 15 per cent of total calories (*Diet, Nutrition and the Prevention of Chronic Disease: Report of a Who Study Group*, WHO Technical Report Series, 1990: 797).

However, recommending such a low fat intake is controversial because of the difficulties in balancing the beneficial lowering of fats with the need for essential nutrients (N Eng J Med, 1997; 337: 562-3; 563-6). Because weight loss is the most usual side effect of such a regime, it is difficult to know, for instance, whether it is the diet per se or the reduction in weight which is responsible for the decrease in cardiac episodes. This question has not been particularly well addressed by Dr Ornish.

It may be that our focus on fat is somewhat lopsided and that equating a healthy diet with restriction is in itself an unhealthy practice. It is unlikely that concerned individuals need consciously to restrict their fat intake. A more positive and automatic way to dramatically reduce fat intake is to increase the intake of nutrient dense foods such as carbohydrates derived from grains, fruits and vegetables, trimming visible fat and/or skin from meat, cutting down on consumption of dairy products and carefully selecting vegetables, fruits and grains on the basis of mineral content.

In one small study, 26 men were randomised into a high fat diet, a fat modified lacto-ovo-vegetarian diet (LOV) or a diet in which 60 per cent of the plant protein in the LOV diet was replaced with lean meat (LM). Compared with the high fat diet, both of the prudent diets significantly lowered blood pressure—though the LOV diet had a greater cholesterol lowering effect than the LM diet (10 per cent versus 5 per cent). The authors concluded that the partial substitution of lean meats for plant protein in the fat-modified diet did not negate its cardiovascular-risk-lowering effect (Am J Clin Nutri, 1989: 50: 280-7).

In another study, the fat content of the diet was reduced from 42 per cent to 25 per cent simply by substituting more nutrient-dense foods. Not surprisingly, the diet of participants ended up being much higher in essential nutrients (Am J Clin Nutri, 1988; 48: 970). Yet another study found that similar dietary counselling produced a 10 per cent decrease in fat intake, with a corresponding increase in vitamin A, beta carotene, vitamin C magnesium iron, folate, vitamin B6, thiamine and riboflavin intake (Am J Clin Nutri, 1991; 53: 890-8).

Such action seems like common sense, but such is the infighting among specialist groups, each wanting the glory of finding the "right" diet to cure heart disease, that only recently did the American Heart Association officially concede that altering the diet is the best way to combat the high blood pressure which can lead to heart failure (American Heart Association Press Release, NR98-4942).

The statement from the AHA came in response to preliminary reports from the Dietary Alternatives to Stop Hypertension, or DASH trial, which found that a salt restricted diet rich in fruits and vegetables, with fat-free or low-fat dairy products produced the greatest reduction in systolic and diastolic blood pressures.

Researchers on the DASH trial studied three diets in 459 adults with mild hypertension and high-normal blood pressure over an eight-week period (Ann Intern Med, 1999; 159: 285-93). The first diet controlled potassium, magnesium and calcium levels and was used as a control. The study diets were either rich in fruits and vegetables or a "combination diet" consisting of fruits, vegetables and either fat-free or low-fat dairy products. All three diets included 7.5 grams of salt daily. Those on the combination diet lowered systolic blood pressure by an average of 5.5 mmHg and diastolic pressure by 3 mmHg. The fruit and vegetable diet lowered systolic by an average of 2.8 mmHg and diastolic pressure by 1.1 mmHg.

The study concluded that to substantially reduce the risk of heart failure, an individual need only to reduce his blood pressure by 5 to

6 mmHg systolic and 2 to 3 mmHg diastolic. This was achieved by the dietary measures in the above study, but other methods are also effective. For some, simply lowering red meat or total meat intake will produce the same results. Exercise has also been shown to help lower blood pressure (Hypertension, 1985; 7: 125-31; Circulation, 1991; 83: 1557-61), though the effects are more long lasting if the individual also practices a sensible eating regime (J Hyperten, 1996; 14: 779-90).

According to some, the success of Ornish's plan simply can't be attributed to low levels of fat and cholesterol. For instance, Dr William Lee Cowden, a cardiologist based in Richardson, Texas, believes that the Ornish regime works because of the low levels of methinoine (an amino acid found in milk, red meat, milk products and a precursor to homocysteine, a free radical generator capable of oxidising cholesterol), as well as a high intake of vegetables and grains. These foods are rich in vitamins B6, C, E and beta carotene, all powerful substances for preventing atherosclerosis (see Burton Goldberg, *Alternative Guide to Heat Disease*, Tiburon, CA: Future Medicine Publishing, 1998).

There is some research evidence to back up this view. One large multicentre European trial found that among men and women younger than age 60, the overall risk of coronary and other vascular disease was 2.2 time higher in those with total plasma homocysteine levels in the top fifth of the normal range, compared to those in the bottom four-fifths (JAMA, 1997; 277: 1775-81).

In another Norwegian study, researchers found that among 587 patients with coronary heart disease, the risk of death after four or five years was also related to high levels of homocysteine. The risk rose from 3.8 per cent in those with the lowest levels (below 9 umol per litre) to 24.7 per cent in those with the highest levels (greater than 15 umol per litre) (N Eng J Med, 1997; 337: 230-6).

Eating For Your Environment

The concept that where you live should influence what you eat is relatively new among Western doctors, though it is well known among practitioners of Oriental medicine. We are beginning to recognise, for instance, that people who live in colder climates need more essential fats. With this understanding it seems prudent to ask whether the very low fat regime promoted by Ornish (and practised in the mostly moderate climate of Northern California) would stand up to a scrutiny in a cold climate.

According to nutrition expert Annemarie Colbin: "A deficiency of fats can create a sensation of inner cold; body functions slow down for lack of warmth and the tissues grow brittle. On the psychospiritual level, too little fat tends to make us joyless and cool. Both excess and deficiency of fats can create a situation which slows down metabolism." (*Food and Healing*, New York: Ballantine, 1996).

Her view is that if such a low-fat diet is adhered to for too long, past the point where it balances the original excess, it may prove harmful. The total lack of added fats in what is mostly a vegetarian diet could cause a deficiency of fat-soluble vitamins such as A and D, as well as of fatty acids essential to metabolism. A certain level of fat intake appears to be necessary to produce the energy necessary for the breakdown of acetates, an intermediate product in metabolic heat production.

"A very low fat diet may be most appropriate in a) warm weather and b) under conditions of metabolic overheating, when people feel warm most of the time and are attracted to cold foods and drinks," she adds. "When these conditions are not present, faithful adherence to such a regime will cause a general cooling of the system, non-physical as well as physical."

Interestingly enough, there is a long-held belief that many people on long-term, very low-fat diets "are notably irritable, fidgety, nervous and depressed" (George Watson, *Nutrition and*

Your Mind, New York: Harper & Row, 1972). Again, such diets are probably best viewed as a short-term, medicinal intervention for very ill people.

To Be or Not to Be a Vegetarian

Many of the claims for the success of Ornish's dietary regime focus on the fact that it is entirely vegetarian. But does a vegetarian regime absolutely prevent heart disease? Of all the foods which are "bad" for the heart, is meat, especially red meat, the worst, and the criticism of it justified?

Surprisingly, no firm conclusions can be made about death from heart disease among vegetarians and meat eaters, though many have tried. Indeed, in many of the studies into diet and heart disease, it is the inclusion of fruits and vegetables, rich in antioxidants such as vitamins A, C and E, rather than the exclusion of meat which has been the decisive factor (BMJ, 1996; 312: 1479-80; 478-81; JAMA, 1995; 274: 1197).

Significantly, when talking about "bad" animal fat, we fail to make the distinction that the fat which is on the meat when purchased does not necessarily end up on the plate or in the mouth. Studies conclude that it is beef fat, not beef itself, which is responsible for a greater risk of heart disease (Am J Clin Nutri, 1990; 19: 491-4). A postal survey, some 20 years ago, quoted by Dr Jeff Wood of the University of Bristol in a recent review article, showed that half the population removed fat before eating the meat. Fat is also lost in cooking. Consequently, in Dr Wood's view, the amount of fat which we consume daily from meat is probably closer to 13 g, rather than 18 g, and that this figure will be under constant review as the meat industry continues to produce animals with less fat on them (Nutri Bull, 1998; 23: 83-7).

Many health-conscious meat eaters are switching to eating lean meat, and recent surveys suggest that lean cuts of meat can be incorporated into a healthy diet without fear of raising levels of fat. Meat eating, like fish eating, does not have to equal gluttony. In the Mediterranean diet, meat is used as a "condiment", and studies confirm that for meat eaters, small amounts are all that is needed to provide optimum nourishment. For instance, in a cross sectional study of 504 young adult meat eaters, those with a low to moderate intake of meat (less than 25th percentile) came closest to meeting dietary recommendations, with 11 per cent of energy from protein, 55 per cent from carbohydrate, 32 per cent from fat, 11 per cent from saturated fatty acids and 264 mg dietary cholesterol (J Am Diet Assoc, 1995; 95: 887-92).

Nevertheless, many researchers believe that they have proven that a vegetarian regime prevents heart disease. In one widely quoted study by Thorogood (BMJ, 1994; 308: 1667-71), 6,115 self-selected non-meat eaters were compared with 5,015 meat eaters over 12 years. So far so good, but the study design allowed a fairly elastic definition as to what constituted a vegetarian. Of the 6,115 vegetarians (referred to in the study as non-meat eaters), 5,728 were defined as those "who did not eat meat or fish, or ate these less than once a week, but did eat eggs or dairy products or both, or vegans". A further 387 were fish eaters who did not eat meat or ate meat less then once a week and who may or may not have eaten eggs or dairy products and fish at least once a week.

By the study's definition, a person who ate meat once every two weeks or once a month would be a vegetarian, and someone who ate fish would be a vegetarian. The study does not comment further on the frequency of meat or fish consumption, but clearly these subjects did receive some of their total nutrition over the study period from fish, and possibly meat, as well as from dairy and eggs.

Other factors such as the "healthy volunteer effect" came into play in this criticised study. Participants were recruited through health food shops, the Vegetarian Society and the media. The vegetarians were then asked to nominate a meat-eating relative or friend to compare themselves with. As one commentator points out, people enthusiastic about their vegetarian lifestyle may have volunteered in order to prove a point (BMJ, 1994; 308: 1671). Equally, they may have chosen friends and relatives who were not as health conscious as themselves in order to drive their point home.

Here the problems of self selection become apparent. The authors did what they could to compensate for these problems but admitted that direct comparison between meat eaters and vegetarians was not really possible. They also concluded that there is no data to justify the advice to "exclude meat from the diet since there are several attributes of a vegetarian diet apart from not eating meat which might reduce the risk."

Some commentators decried that Thorogood's study did not last long enough to justify her conclusion that the death rate is significantly different. Had Thorogood extended the study another five years, they argued, the "healthy volunteer effect" would have worn off and figures would be more reliable (BMJ, 1994; 309: 955). Certainly, when other researchers have compared death from all causes in vegetarians and non-vegetarians, the death rate did not alter appreciably after exclusion of early deaths (during the first years of observation). This suggests that the self-selected vegetarians, who are often used in such studies, are probably at no greater risk than their health-conscious, meat-eating peers (Am J Clin Nutr, 1982; 36: 873-7).

In another study, Thorogood undertook a re-analysis of a group originally studied by Michael L Burr and associates (Am J Clin Nutri, 1982; 36: 873-7; Am J Clin Nutri, 1988; 48: 830-2). What she and her colleagues found was that the gap between the death rate of vegetarians and meat eaters narrowed as time went on—and had even halved in just two years (from 30 per cent to 15 per cent). The original aim of this analysis was to test the hypothesis that daily consumption of wholemeal bread (as an indicator of a high fibre diet) and a vegetarian diet was associated with a reduction in mortality from ischaemic heart disease. However, the reduction in mortality associated with both of these dietary factors was not significant. Across the board, the only significant factor in lowering mortality from all causes was daily consumption of fruit. Health consciousness, not vegetarianism, was the decisive factor (BMJ, 1996; 313: 775-9).

Their main findings were consistent with other studies showing that an increased intake of foods rich in vitamin C and beta-carotene are the significant factors in reducing death from heart disease and stroke (Am J Epidemiol, 1995, 142: 1269-78; Epidemiol, 1992, 3: 194-202; BMJ, 1990; 300: 771-3; Am J Epidemiol, 1994; 139: 1180-9; Lancet, 1983; i: 1191-3; JAMA, 1995; 273: 1113-7).

The idea that it is not the exclusion of meat but what you eat and other lifestyle factors is underscored, for instance, by studies of the Yi people of China. The Yi are a lean bodied people, but they are not vegetarians. Their diet consists mainly of rice, a little meat, and lots of fresh fruit and vegetables, as well as grains such as buckwheat and oats (Am J Clin Nutri, 1995; 61: 366-72). Studies of the Yi's migratory habits suggest that it is not diet but lifestyle that affects their long-term health. When the Yi move to an urban setting, they begin drinking alcohol more heavily. Alcohol use was shown to have the most significant effect on the development of hypertension—responsible for 33 per cent of cases (Hypertension, 1993; 22: 365-70).

Besides fresh fruits and vegetables, including even a small amount of fish in the diet can bring significant improvements in heart health, according to several studies. In one 1960 study, dietary histories were taken on healthy men, with special attention to fish consumption. At the start of the study, 20 per cent of the men ate no fish; the rest ate on average three-quarters of an ounce per day.

The men were followed for 20 years, during which time seventy-eight died of coronary disease. The researchers concluded that the risk of heart attack was inversely related to the amount of fish consumed daily—the more fish the men ate, the lower their risk (N Eng J Med, 1985; 312: 1205-9). In this study, eating just an ounce of fish a day reduced the risk of heart disease by 50 per cent. According to the authors, the most likely reason for this protection was the influence of the long-chain fatty acid eicosapentaenoic acid (EPA) on clotting tendencies.

In the same issue of the Journal, (N Eng J Med, 1985; 312: 1210-6) a smaller Dutch study of fish consumption placed 20 patients on three successive, controlled diets, which differed only in the kind of fat included. The first diet was low in fat and cholesterol, and contained no fish oil, and the second contained fish oil (both in fish and supplements), amounting to 20 to 30 per cent of daily calories. The third diet substituted an equal amount of polyunsaturated vegetable oils for the fish oil of the second diet.

In every patient, blood-fat levels dropped while on the fish oil-rich diets. After just four weeks, triglyceride levels fell an average of 64 per cent in those who had moderately high triglyceride levels at the start of the study; for those with severely high levels, they fell an average of 79 per cent. Cholesterol levels in these groups fell 27 per cent and 45 per cent, respectively.

Surprisingly, when the patients were taken off the fish oil-rich diet and placed on a diet rich in polyunsaturated vegetable oils, levels of both triglycerides and cholesterol rose considerably. While vegetable oils are known to reduce these blood fats considerably, they proved far less effective than fish oils.

Polyunsaturated fats

Diets with high percentages of polyunsaturated fats have been demonstrated to lower cholesterol levels, but without reducing the

93

risk of heart disease or death. In fact, some theoretical studies question whether this diet doesn't actually increase arterial plaque formation (Lancet, 1994; 344: 1195-6).

According to authors Petr Skrabanek and James McCormick, some large-scale studies have examined the effects of the standard WHO diet—limiting fat intake to 30 per cent of total dietary intake, with no more than 10 per cent each of saturated, polyunsaturated and monounsaturated fats. After 828,000 man-years of study, they wrote, there were four fewer deaths in 10,000 men per year. "Such a small difference is well within the limits of chance" (P Skrabanek and J McCormick, *Follies and Fallacies in Medicine*, Glasgow: Tarragon Press, 1990: 95).

In the end, individuals searching for the single right diet which will lower their risk of heart disease or prevent existing disease from worsening are likely to be disappointed. The reasons for developing heart disease are as numerous and individual as the people who develop it. What works for one individual may not work for another, and how one person measures success may be completely different from how another measures it.

There is evidence for and against almost every kind of eating plan and lifestyle modification. Dean Ornish has achieved reasonable results with his experimental group. For some, it may literally have been a lifesaver. But for others, it is simply too extreme and best left as an intervention for those at the highest risk. Finding the appropriate diet for you is something which only you can do. Only you live in your body and only you can say what feels right. In the end it may be a mixture of approaches, culled from your own research, that suits you best. Indeed, given how little we still know about the mechanics of heart disease, the mix-and-match approach may be just as scientific as any official or prescribed plan.

CHAPTER 7

CHELATION THERAPY

Chelation therapy is claimed to be a safer alternative to surgery and drug therapies. Its name comes from how it works; molecules called chelators are employed which have the ability to target stray atoms and chelate, or chemically seize them, holding on tightly. Their particular speciality is to remove metals from the body.

One of the most common agents used is ethylenediamine tetra-acetic acid, or EDTA, a cluster of four acetic acid groups with two nitrogen atoms. Whenever this cluster bumps up against a metal ion, the molecules form a tight ring around the metal.

EDTA has been licensed by the US FDA since the 1950s for patients with toxic metal overload, particularly of lead, mercury and aluminium, or nutritional metals, such as copper or iron, located in the wrong place in the body. However, one of the byproducts of chelation is to improve the metabolic and circulatory function of arteries formerly blocked by plaque. Some believe that accumulation of heavy metals in the body, as well as substances like calcium, is responsible for atherosclerosis. By removing metals and calcium deposits from the body, chelation therapy removes its source.

Chelation involves up to 30 infusions of EDTA via a slow drip into the bloodstream, usually given twice a week. As EDTA moves through a patient's blood system, it binds with artery-clogging deposits, and as the acid passes out of the body, so the deposits are excreted.

Many organisations in the US and UK have enthusiastically taken up chelation therapy—notably the Arterial Disease Clinic in London and Lancashire and the American College of Advancement in Medicine (ACAM), which provides a protocol for chelation therapy use in the US as well as a list of participating clinics.

To date, there have been no scientific (that is, randomised, double-blind) studies proving the benefit of chelation therapy.

Nevertheless, the American Institute of Medical Prevention (AIMP) holds a permit issued by the FDA to investigate chelation therapy for future licensing. The AIMP is also co-sponsor of ongoing FDA-approved studies of EDTA chelation therapy to treat arteriosclerosis.

A supposedly scientific study, conducted by a Danish vascular surgeon and his colleagues, apparently showed that intravenous disodium EDTA is not effective in the treatment of hardening of the arteries (Am J Surgery, 1991; 162: 122-5; J Internal Med, 1992; 231: 261-7).

A flawed study

However, AIMP's president James Frackelton, writing in the Townsend Letter for Doctors (July 1992), maintains that the Danish study contains a number of serious flaws.

For one thing, the Danes used disodium EDTA, which is "less effective" than the magnesium EDTA used in the US and in the FDA-licensed studies says Frackelton. And although the study claimed to be double-blind, "the investigators themselves admitted that the study was not properly blinded," he charges.

"The investigators instructed patients to chew and swallow a mineral supplement containing a substantial amount of iron during the course of each infusion. . . . EDTA has a very high affinity for iron, and the iron in those tablets would have reacted irreversibly with a larger percentage of the infused EDTA, thus neutralising any potential benefit," he adds.

Positive results with chelation therapy come mostly from clinical observational studies by private physicians. In a retrospective study of 470 patients given chelation therapy, 80 to 91 per cent demonstrated improvements. "Of 92 patients referred for surgical intervention, only 10 required ultimate surgery after or during their chelation therapy," said the report (J Advancement Med, Fall 1993).

A similar study of 77 elderly patients with narrowed arteries in the lower extremities showed that intravenous EDTA chelation therapy with multivitamin supplementation improved arterial blood flow significantly after 60 days and 26 infusions (J Holistic Med, Spring/Summer 1985).

Most significantly, an analysis of 19 articles on chelation therapy covering nearly 23,000 patients showed that 87 per cent demonstrated improved cardiovascular function by objective testing (J Advancement Med, Fall 1993).

Helping chronic lung disorders

Chelation therapy has also been used successfully to improve chronic lung disorders (Health Consciousness, April 1990); to treat cancer, where in one study it reduced mortality by 90 per cent during an 18-year follow up (J Advancement Med, Spring/Summer 1989); and to remove the toxic effect of aluminium in kidney dialysis patients (Lancet, 1988; 1: 1009-14).

The attempts of the cardiac establishment to discredit chelation therapy were fuelled by the deaths of 13 patients at Meadowbrook Hospital in Belle Chasse, Louisiana in the mid-1970s.

The bad press began when by John David Spence, a professed opponent of chelation therapy from Victoria Hospital in London, Ontario, Canada, conducted an audit of the Meadowbrook

Hospital for the US Department of Health, Education and Welfare.

Chelation therapy can cause kidney damage and so should not be used on people with kidney disease. Any patient placed on intravenous EDTA should be carefully monitored for kidney damage.

However, at Meadowbrook, Spence found that a number of patients continued to receive EDTA, even after their kidney tests showed results above the hospital's cut-off point for continuing with the therapy. A number of patients subsequently died of kidney failure. Patients with congestive heart failure had been given a higher solution of EDTA than they were supposed to have. Other patients weren't being closely monitored.

In defending the late Dr Ray Evers, who headed Meadowbrook at the time, Dr Michael B Schachter, president of the ACAM, says that Dr Evers often accepted patients with advanced disease whom conventional medicine had virtually given up on. He also maintained: "Virtually no deaths are reported from EDTA chelation therapy when the ACAM protocol is followed" (Townsend Lett for Docs, Aug/Sept 1991).

Nevertheless, Spence's audit does demonstrate that chelation can be dangerous if the therapy is administered without strict adherence to protocol.

If you do wish to try chelation therapy, it is vital that you go to a highly experienced doctor or clinic which strictly follows ACAM protocol. It's also important that you follow a full programme for cardiovascular disease, including an optimal diet, appropriate nutritional supplements, a regular exercise programme and stress management.

The Arterial Disease Clinic will accept all victims in any condition, be they gangrene sufferers, stroke victims, or bypass and angioplasty failures. Nevertheless, a worrying aspect of chelation is the tendency to promote it almost as a "feel-good" treatment: the

Arterial Disease Clinic's promotional literature cites one case study that gave the (incorrect) impression that a young man had chelation therapy simply to allow him to run faster. Other doctors are beginning to talk about chelation as a just-in-case treatment for those with a family history of heart disease.

Chelation therapy is also very expensive. A 30-infusion treatment will cost around £3000, although some doctors offer an "abbreviated" form of the course for mild cases at a reduced rate. (Bear in mind, however, that it costs you, the government or insurers three times that to do bypass surgery.)

If you are considering chelation therapy, Dr Wayne Perry of London's Wimpole Street, advises:

• Check that the doctor is experienced in the practice and will be following the ACAM protocol. (The drugs used in chelation therapy are widely available, and there is nothing to stop any doctor from offering this treatment.)

• Check that he will be monitoring your kidney function before and after chelation.

• Find out in advance exactly what drugs you will be receiving and do your own research to make sure you are happy about the proposed treatment.

In the UK, the best bet is to contact the Arterial Disease Clinic in London (Tel: 0171 935 6604) or Lancashire (01942 676 617). Individual doctors carrying out chelation include Dr Hugh Cox at the Sozo Clinic in Aylesbury, Bucks, Dr Fritz Schellander at the Liongate Clinic in Tunbridge Wells, and Dr Patrick Kingsley in Osgathorpe, Leicestershire. In the US, the best bet is to contact the ACAM (23121 Verdugo Dr, Suite 204, Laguna Hills, CA 92653, Tel: 949 583 7666) for recommendations on clinics following ACAM protocol.

CHAPTER 8

THE ROLE OF CONNECTEDNESS

Modern medicine has never convincingly answered the question: what causes heart disease in the first place?

Dr Dean Ornish has collected copious research on the various causes of heart disease. He has discovered that while smoking, obesity, a sedentary lifestyle and high-fat diet are important risk factors, they only account for half of all heart disease. In Dr Ornish's research, none appears more important than isolation—from other people, from our own feelings and from a higher source.

In trials in San Francisco and Eastern Finland, of the nearly 20,000 people observed for up to nine years, those who were lonely and socially isolated were two to three times more likely to die from heart disease and other causes than those who felt connected to others. These results occurred independently of risk factors such as high cholesterol level or high blood pressure, smoking and family history (Am J Epidemiol, 1979; 109: 186-204; Am J Epidemiol, 1988; 128: 370-80). The usual suspects have less to do with having a heart attack than loneliness.

Dying of a broken heart

Studies of other populations, such as Japanese-Americans, demonstrate—that social networks and social support protect them against heart disease—regardless of whether they smoke or suffer from high blood pressure (Am J Epidemiol, 1983; 117: 384-96). In another study among more than 200 elderly, healthy adults, those with good support networks had lower blood cholesterol levels and higher levels of immune functions than those without this emotional support. Again, how much you smoked or what you ate didn't seem to have as much bearing on your heart as whether you were lonely or isolated.

Although animal studies cannot be extrapolated to humans, researchers conducting heart studies on rabbits have been flabbergasted to find that among animals given high cholesterol-producing diets, those who were petted by researchers developed less cardiovascular disease than those who were in cages out of reach and left alone (Science, 1980; 208: 1475-6).

In other words, whether in animals or humans, a high cholesterol diet doesn't have as much to do with heart disease as a lack of love.

This lends a certain credence to the view that how we get ill is a metaphor for our lives; many people suffering heart problems literally die from a broken heart.

Depression after heart attack has also been recognised as having an influence on patients' survival rate. Its impact is at least equivalent to that of left ventricular dysfunction and a history of previous heart attack (JAMA, 1993; 270: 819-25). Again, this effect has been shown to be independent of the severity of the patient's condition (JAMA, 1993; 270: 1819-25; Circulation, 1995; 91: 999-1005).

Depressed patients experience physiological changes such as a decrease in the variability of their heart rates (J Psychosom Res, 1988; 32: 159-64; Am J Cardiol, 1987; 59: 256-62). Studies also show that the hormone serotonin not only plays a major part in the development of depression, but also influences the formation of blood clots (Pharmocol, 1991; 17: S6-12).

And of course, the low cholesterol regimes which heart attack patients are often put on only exacerbate the problem; men with low cholesterol levels are three times as likely to commit suicide (see chapter 1).

Unremitting stress caused by living in a cramped, unnatural way also has been fingered as a major culprit in heart disease. Even in the animal kingdom, when animals are placed in competitive environments with constant power struggles and a confusing social hierarchy—in short, the typical dog-eat-dog environment of your average work place—the animals develop heart problems.

Stress has more to do with heart disease than diet or other risk factors (Arteriosclerosis, 1982; 2: 359-68). In humans, chronic stress causes the body to overproduce cortisol, our "fight or flight" stress hormone, which increases the formation of arterial plaque.

Dr Ornish has also found studies showing that people who are self-absorbed, cynical and hostile to the world after feeling isolated also tend to die from a heart attack. One study actually found that the number of times a person used words like "I", "me" and "mine" in an ordinary conversation multiplied the risk of a person's dying from heart disease (Psychosom Med, 1986; 48: 187-99)!

"Anything that promotes a sense of isolation leads to chronic stress and, often, to illnesses like heart disease," writes Ornish (*Reversing Heart Disease*, Century, 1990). "Conversely, anything that leads to a real intimacy and feelings of connection can be healing. . ." By connection, Dr Ornish means both connection with others, our feelings, our inner peace, and also with a higher, spiritual force.

The body-mind connection

Some of the most successful alternative treatments for heart disease concentrate on techniques which will remove stress and foster internal connectedness. Dozens of studies have examined whether stress management has a bearing on high blood pressure. One of the best studies, which had a four-year follow up, attempted to show that reducing stress is one of the most important lifestyle changes you can make. In the study of nearly 200 patients, all the subjects were given information sheets on modifying such bad habits as smoking and consuming too much animal fats in the diet (they were not placed on any diet or monitored to see if they followed through on the recommendations). However, half the group were also given lessons in breathing exercises, relaxation, meditation and managing stress.

The group practising relaxation recorded a significantly greater reduction in blood pressure than the others, and this difference was maintained over four years. Most strikingly, although there were no differences between the two groups in terms of cholesterol levels, the group not given the relaxation lessons suffered a much higher incidence of ischaemic heart disease, fatal heart attack and narrowing of heart blood artery flow than the group who meditated (BMJ [Clin Res], 1985; 13: 1103-6).

In another study, 34 patients with hypertension who were trained in yoga were able to lower their blood pressure from an average of 168/100 to 141/84 mmHg. The untreated group were then given yoga training, at which point their blood pressure also fell to levels similar to those of the other group (Lancet, 1975; 2: 93-5).

The yoga practice of right-nostril breathing, otherwise known as *surya anuloma viloma pranayama* (SAV), was assessed in a crossover study to investigate its effect on blood pressure. After the SAV session, there was a significant decrease in systolic blood pressure, a 17 per cent increase in oxygen consumption, and a 45.7 per cent decrease in pulse rates (J Alt Comp Med Res Paradigm Pract Policy, 1996; 2: 479-84).

Transcendental Meditation (TM) is one of the most effective non-drug approaches to reducing high blood pressure. A study of 127 men over 55 concluded that it is as effective as antihypertensive drugs. Each individual was randomly divided into three groups: one received TM, another was taught Progressive Muscle Relaxation (PMR—similar to Autogenic Training) and the third was simply given advice on diet and lifestyle. After three months, both the TM and PMR groups reduced their blood pressure significantly, but TM was found to be twice as effective as PMR, reducing systolic blood pressure by 10.7 points (Hypertension, 1995; 26: 820-7).

TM can also lower cholesterol in patients with high cholesterol, as it has been shown to do in one group when compared to matched controls over an 11-month period (J Hum Stress, 1979; 5: 24-7).

In yet another study, patients with coronary artery disease practising TM had a 14.7 per cent increase in exercise tolerance, an 11.7 per cent increase in maximal workload and a significant reduction in blood pressure (Am J Cardiol, 1996; 77: 867-70).

One study attempted to determine the actual physiological effects of TM or yoga. It found that among a group of patients who shared similar behaviours, including exercise, and a family history of hypertension, those practising meditation recorded a lower percentage of the cells that stimulate the body's "fight or flight" mechanism (J Psychosom Research, 1990; 34: 29-33).

But in many other instances, relaxation techniques haven't worked at all (BMJ, 1990; 300: 1368-72), or have only worked in a minority of cases (J Psychosom Res, 1987; 31: 453).

Much appears to depend on which types of techniques you choose; overall, yoga and TM—disciplines which attempt to put you in touch with your own spirituality, as well as relax you—have outperformed techniques like stress management and biofeedback, which concentrate only on relaxing the body.

Other studies have been able to quantify the power of love in preventing heart disease. One study showed that old people with pets have lower blood pressure than those without; both the interactions with the pet and the pleasure derived from stroking it were thought to be responsible (J Behav Med, 1988; 11: 509-17).

There is also evidence that suggestibility plays a part in lowering blood pressure. In one study, a group of patients told their blood pressure would lower with relaxation actually did have it fall by 7 or 8 points, whereas those told the techniques would have no effect only registered half that change in blood pressure (Hypertension, 1993; 11: 293-6). In another study, high blood pressure was completely eliminated during hypnosis, regardless of whether or not a patient was on antihypertensive drugs (Am J Clin Hypn, 1973; 16: 75-83).

CHAPTER 9
PROVEN ALTERNATIVE
TREATMENTS

In the view of modern medicine, heart disease is its deadliest and most intractable adversary, one that can only be vanquished by the most powerfully suppressive drugs, the most sophisticated surgery, the greatest state-of-the-art technology. In the view of most doctors, attempting to treat this disease by alternative medicine is akin to attempting to cure cancer with a facial.

But this view of heart disease ignores clear scientific evidence demonstrating that many alternative remedies are far more potent in preventing or treating heart disease than all of medicine's most sophisticated armaments put together.

Homoeopathy

It is always difficult to subject individualised treatments like homoeopathy to a scientific trial, for the simple reason that classical homoeopaths tailor the treatment to the individual constitution.

Nevertheless, two good scientific trials provide some evidence that homoeopathy can be used to prevent or treat heart disease. In one controlled, double-blind trial of 32 elderly hypertensive patients confined to bed at one of two nursing homes, half were given *Baryta carbonica* (barium chloride) and the other half a placebo. Among the group as a whole, those taking the homoeopathic remedy didn't show much improvement. However, the four subjects who'd been considered sensitive, in homoeopathic terms, had strongly positive results (Brit Homeop J, 1987; 76: 114-9).

In another study, 42 patients on antihypertensive medication were divided into two groups. Ten were given a placebo and advised to reduce weight, decrease salt intake and engage in exercise, relaxation, yoga and meditation. The remaining 32 patients were given homoeopathic drugs alone. Among the diet-exercise-relaxation group, 60 per cent had no improvement in blood pressure. But among the homoeopathic group, 75 per cent showed improvement in blood pressure, and within 60 days, 86 per cent had been able to gradually taper their hypertensive drugs (Br Homeop J, 1987; 76: 120-1). This particular trial used a variety of homoeopathic remedies, including *Adrenalin 30, Adrenalin 200, Eel Serum 6* and *Baryta Mur 30*.

Herbal medicine

For general prevention of arterial damage, perhaps the most studied remedy is *Ginkgo biloba*, a herb from the Maidenhair tree. *Ginkgo* is known to help with respiratory complaints, like asthma, but it's also known as a circulatory stimulant which increases blood flow to the brain. Patients with peripheral arteriopathy of the lower extremities (blood doesn't flow well to the lower extremities) also benefit from *Ginkgo biloba*.

In one double-blind French trial, conducted for more than a year, 36 patients were given the herb and matched against 35 patients who were given a placebo. *Ginkgo biloba* was found to give significantly greater pain relief and helped patients walk longer distances, than placebo. *Ginkgo* has also been found to "thin" the blood in patients suffering from arteriosclerosis who were experimentally given blood-clotting substances (Wiener Medizinische Wochenschrift, 1989; 139: 92-4).

Besides *Ginkgo*, several multi-herbal preparations have excellent success rates in alleviating arterial problems. *Abana*, a preparation from Ayurvedic Medicine which contains a variety of herbs and minerals, has been shown to affect blood pressure among 80 per cent of patients in a study comparing it to medication (Japan Heart J, 1990; 31: 829-35). The Ayurvedic herbal mixtures MAK-4 and MAK-5, both rich in antioxidants, were shown to reduce total cholesterol, triglycerides and LDL cholesterol in patients with high blood-fat levels, without changing HDL ("good") cholesterol levels (Am J Med Sci, 1997; 314: 303-10). *Padma 28*, a Tibetan herbal combination of 28 herbs (which must be made up by a practitioner of Tibetan medicine), has been shown to help poor circulation in the legs. Researchers were actually able to record a number of biochemical improvements in the blood (Fibrinolysis, 1994; 8: 47-9; Forschende Kompolementarmedizin, 1994; 1: 1-13).

For angina, bromelain, the enzyme from the stem of the pineapple plant, has been shown to reduce attacks (Erfahungsheilkunde, 1978; 5: 274-5), as can *Khella* (*Ammi visnaga*), an ancient medicinal plant (N Eng J Med, 1951; 244: 315-21).

Ammi visnaga is a wild member of the carrot family that grows in Africa. There is good evidence that it improves blood supply to the heart muscle and improves the overall efficiency and chemistry of the heart (R F Weiss, *Herbal Medicine*, Ab Arcanum, 1988). The extract visnadine is available as a branded German product called Carduben.

Herbalists know that extract of hawthorn berries, leaves or flowering tops (*Crataegus pinnatifida*) is the "food for the heart" par excellence. They believe that it increases blood flow to the heart muscles and can restore a normal heartbeat, and it has been proven to reduce angina (J Trad Chin Med, 1984; 4: 293-4). A landmark German trial in 1994 confirmed that it could lower blood pressure as well as regulate the heartbeat.

In a review of recent studies, two researchers have confirmed that hawthorn can also be useful for treating early-stage congestive heart failure, and without any noticeable side effects (Fortschritte der Medizin, 1996; 114: 27-9). It has also been proven effective in several trials in treating heart arrhythmias (irregular heart beat) (Planta Med, 1977; 43: 209-39; 313-22).

Another good herb is extract of barberry root (*Berberis vulgaris*), proven to treat or prevent irregular heartbeats (Chung Hua Hsin Hsueh Kuan Ping Tsa Chih, 1990; 18: 155-6). Berberine, an alkaloid extracted from the roots and bark of various plants—such as goldenseal, barberry root bark and Oregon grape root—may also help lower and regulate the heart rate of patients with ventricular tachyarrhythmias (rapid heart beat) (Chung Hua Hsin Hsueh Kuan Ping Tsa Chih, 1990; 18: 190).

Fenugreek can reduce cholesterol levels (Phytother Res, 1991; 5: 145-7), as can milk thistle (Acta Med Hung, 1989; 46: 289-95). Ginger has also been known to thin the blood (Med Hypotheses, 1986; 20: 271), and there's some evidence that artichoke extract can help normalise blood cholesterol levels (Arzneim Forsch, 1975; 25: 1311-4).

A number of Chinese herbs also have proof of exerting profound effects on the heart. *Andrographis paniculata nees* has been found useful in preventing restenosis (reclogging of the arteries) after angioplasty (J Tongi Med Univ, 1993; 13: 193-8). *Astragalic membranaceus*, another Chinese herb, can help preserve cardiac function (Chung-Kuo Hung Hsi i Chieh Ho Tsa Chih, 1995; 15: 141-3). Although other Chinese herbs claim to help heart conditions, all such studies are derived from Chinese journals, which tend to publish uncritical research.

Terminalia arjuna bark—the principal Ayurvedic herb for heart problems—has been shown to help heart patients. It was used in a double-blind, cross-over trial on 12 patients with refractory congestive heart failure. Compared to similar patients given a placebo, patients treated with 500 mg of powdered *Terminalia arjuna* showed a decrease in symptoms of heart failure. Heart function improved and both systolic and diastolic blood pressure measurements decreased (Int J Cardiol, 1995; 49: 191-9). This herb may also be useful for unblocking arteries in heart patients. In another study of patients with either ischaemic cardiomyopathy—heart disease due to inadequate blood flow—or those with angina who'd suffered a heart attack, both the control group and the experimental group (who took both conventional treatment and *Terminalia arjuna*) experienced a significant reduction in angina. But only the *arjuna* group showed improvement in the flow of blood through the congested left ventricle. Long-term dosage with *arjuna* showed no side effects on the kidneys, liver or blood systems (Indian Heart J, 1997; 49: 507-10).

Spiritual healing

Besides the more conventional body-mind techniques, many alternative spiritual therapies are considered useful for heart patients. This includes therapies involving an intermediary healing another, either through touch or prayer.

One famous study involved two groups of patients in a coronary care unit, about half of whom were prayed for by a group of Christians outside the hospital, while the other half received normal hospital care only. Nobody in the trial knew if he or she was being prayed for. When compared to evaluations taken before the trial, those who were prayed for had a less severe heart condition after the trial had finished. Those who were not prayed for needed more ventilatory assistance, antibiotics and diuretics than those in the treatment group (South Med J, 1988; 91: 826-9).

The effects of praying or healing extend beyond those of simple feel-good activities. For instance, playing music or suggestion tapes hasn't been shown to have any effect in intensive-care situations (J Clin Hypnosis, 1995; 37: 32-42).

One study of faith healing—which seeks to generate a person's own self-healing capacities—found that patients who pursued complementary approaches while recovering from coronary surgery, especially prayer and exercise, experienced significantly improved psychological recovery (J Altern Comp Med, 1997; 3: 343-53).

Those therapies considered "paranormal" have achieved little success in healing so-called cardiac risk factors. One test of paranormal healing tried to determine if the laying on of hands could reduce blood pressure in patients suffering from hypertension. Patients were randomised into one of three treatment groups: those given paranormal healing by laying on of hands, those given paranormal healing at a distance, and controls without any healing. Although blood pressure fell in all three groups, the researchers could not say that paranormal healing was the cause, as those receiving no treatment at all fared equally well (BMJ, 1988; 296: 1491-4).

Another group of hypertensive patients was enlisted for a double-blind trial of remote mental healing, involving 96 patients and eight healers. Those being healed had a significant improvement in their systolic blood pressure levels afterwards, although there were no major differences in diastolic blood pressure and pulse. Four of the healers had a 92.3 per cent improvement ratio in their group of patients, compared with a 73.7 per cent improvement for the control group (those not receiving any treatment) (Med Hypotheses, 1982; 8: 481-90).

This study suggests that success depends on the skill and experience of the healers.

Acupuncture

Acupuncture also has a place in the treatment of cardiac disease. Most studies have examined its role in alleviating the pain of angina. Thus far, the results of tests are mixed, although there are at least two successful studies.

In one randomised trial, where half the subjects received acupuncture and the other half a sham treatment, the patients receiving acupuncture were able to increase the work capacity of their hearts significantly (J Clin Epidemiol, 1990; 43: 1191-9). In tests on angina patients in Denmark, acupuncture was found to reduce the length of an attack by 10 per cent, reduce nitroglycerin consumption by 58 per cent and reduce the severity of the attack by 38 per cent. Patients were also better able to exercise (Acupunct Electrother Res, 1995; 20: 101-16).

Acupuncture is also helpful in hypertension; in one study, it showed immediate effect among all patients and a longer-term effect among two-thirds (J Trad Chin Med, 1992; 12: 133-6).

In Western terms, the good effects of acupuncture may be traced in part to its effect on the blood. One study compared the blood biochemical parameters of a group of volunteers undergoing acupuncture to a set of controls and found a significant increase of free fatty acids concentration. This accords with what we know about the beneficial effects of omega-3 fatty acids in protecting the heart (Anaesthetist, 1976; 25: 235-8).

There is also solid evidence that the Chinese therapy Qigong, involving a series of moving and static exercises designed to cultivate energy, can be useful with patients with hypertension (J Trad Chinese Med, 1987; 7: 169-70).

Alternative treatments at a glance

For angina:
- Consider acupuncture, which can alleviate pain and reduce the length and severity of a heart attack.
- Consider taking 125 to 450 mg of the pineapple enzyme bromelain, three times a day.
- Hawthorn extract, *Khella* or extract of barberry root can alleviate symptoms.

For hypertension:
- Learn a relaxation technique, particularly yoga or TM.
- Herbal preparations, such as *Abana*, can help lower blood pressure, as can hawthorn extract.
- The Chinese therapy Qigong can be useful.
- Hypnosis by a qualified, experienced practitioner can lower blood pressure.
- Homoeopathic remedies such as *Baryta carbonica*, *Adrenalin 30*, *Adrenalin 200*, *Eel Serum 6* and *Baryta Mur 30* (or those personalised for you) can bring down blood pressure.
- Find a healer with proven success in lowering blood pressure and improving heart disease, and consider acupuncture.

For ischaemia, particularly in the legs:
- *Ginkgo biloba* may reduce pain and increase walking distance.
- The Tibetan herbal preparation *Padma 28* can improve poor circulation in the legs.
- Extract of *Ammi visnaga* may help increase blood supply to the heart.

For heart failure:
- The herb *Terminalia arjuna* can help with symptoms.
- Extract of hawthorn is a useful treatment with no side effects.

For high cholesterol and avoiding atherosclerosis:
- Herbal extracts of artichoke, fenugreek seeds, ginger, gugulipids, milk thistle, malabar tamarind and silymarin may help lower blood cholesterol levels.
- Eggplant may help to inhibit the furring up of arteries.
- Ayurvedic herbal preparations MAK-4 and MAK-5 reduce

the "bad" cholesterol without affecting the "good" cholesterol.

- TM may help reduce cholesterol levels.

If you have already had a heart attack:

- Herbs like red ginseng and *Astragalus membranaceus* may be good after heart failure.

With heart surgery:

- Pray or have someone pray consistently for you.
- Acupuncture will help to alleviate pain and regulate your heart afterward.
- The herb *Andrographis paniculata nees* can help to prevent restenosis after coronary angioplasty.

If you are a heart patient of any sort:

- Work on ending isolation from your own feelings, from other people and from a higher being. Making friends, expressing your feelings, taking care of a pet, praying or developing your own spirituality may save your life.
- Engage in regular (but non-competitive) exercise.

CHAPTER 10

THE HEALTHY
HEART DIET

In an editorial in the Journal of Nutritional Medicine, nutritional medicine pioneer Dr Stephen Davies once examined whether the current twentieth century Western diet was adequate to meet the current challenges of our environment.

The point he made in great detail was that people haven't changed much over 40,000 years, but, at least here in the West, our diet has (J Nut Med, 1991; 2: 227-47). He quotes Eaton and Konner, writing about Palaeolithic nutrition in the New England Journal of Medicine (1985; 312: 283-9): "Even the development of agriculture 10,000 years ago has apparently had a minimal effect on our genes. Certain haemaglobinopathies and retention of intestinal lactase into adulthood are 'recent' genetic evolutionary trends, but few other examples are known."

In other words, the business of food might be modern and industrial, but our old-fashioned stomachs are still designed for a hunting and gathering diet. At that time, we consumed 21 per cent of our total dietary energy from fats, 34 per cent from protein and 45.7 g of fibre (with cholesterol intake a whopping 591 mg compared to the usual recommendations these days of 300 mg). Today, the average UK male takes in 37.6 per cent of his dietary energy from fats and 14.1 per cent from protein, with only 24.9 g of fibre and 390 mg of cholesterol. By modern day standards, cave men should have been dropping like flies.

But clearly, fat is a very small part of the story. Numerous studies show that when more primitive populations begin to consume a Western diet, they start dying of heart attacks. One article showed that when a population of Mexican Indians with virtually no heart problems went on a typical Western diet for two months, they dramatically increased their blood fat levels (New Eng J Med, 1991; 325: 1704-8).

But the main difference between what they're eating and what we're eating is not meat or fats, but whole foods. The culprit appears to be the large-scale adulterating, or "dismembering", of everything we put in our mouths.

One of the results of modern agribusiness with its domestication of animals, birds and fish, says Davies, is a substantial lowering of the consumption of essential fatty acids (EFAs), which we now know are vital to a healthy immune system. "Intensive livestock farming of pigs and chickens in particular, where the animals are kept indoors in overcrowded conditions, is associated with nutrient deficiencies of these animals," writes Stephen Davies.

"Food processing and refining techniques further compromise nutrient content, as do intensive farming techniques which result in soil demineralisation. The agrochemical and other environmental pollutants find their way into the food chain, and further disrupt the nutrient value of the foods, and stress our detoxification. . . mechanisms" (J Nut Med, 1991; 2: 227-47).

Today's meat business makes liberal use of steroids, antibiotics, tranquillisers and beta-blockers. Agrochemical industry currently employs pesticides, herbicides, rodenticides, fungicides and nitrate fertilisers.

Current food processing refines wheat and sugar, which reduces trace mineral and vitamin content, as do current storage methods, food irradiation, and the addition of some 3,794 food additives, colourings, sweeteners, texture modifiers and preservatives. The refining of sugar also increases blood fats and lowers the strength of the immune system.

What Davies is really saying is that much degenerative illness—such as coronary heart disease—could be, in large part, failure of our bodies to catch up with this virtual revolution in what now constitutes "food". In other words, the culprit isn't necessarily cholesterol or sugar or any one food, but rather the very means we now use to grow, collect, sell and prepare what we serve at the table.

The Healthy Heart Diet

Even if you've already had a heart attack, there is much that you can do for yourself. Diet and lifestyle are factors within an individual's control. There is plenty of research to show that eating raw foods can prevent heart attacks. Two or three servings a day of fruit, high in vitamin C and soluble fibre, can reduce the risk of heart disease by as much as 25 per cent (N Eng J Med, 1987; 316: 235-40; Am J Epidemiol 1987; 126: 1093-102; Am J Epidemiol, 1994; 139: S47). One 17-year study showed that people who eat fresh fruit every day are less likely to suffer from heart problems, with 24 per cent less fatal heart disease, a 32 per cent reduction in death from stroke and, overall, a 21 per cent lower mortality rate (BMJ, 1996; 313: 775-79). The same study revealed that if you have a raw salad every day, your risk of fatal heart disease is lowered by 26 per cent.

The following is a summary of suggestions for a healthy heart diet, compiled from the research of a variety of nutritionists, such as Drs Leo Galland and Stephen Davies. However, it goes without saying that anyone suffering from heart disease should not embark on a diet without regularly consulting an experienced nutritional specialist.

Eat whole foods

Because most dietary recommendations are faddish, your safest bet is to follow some of the basic dietary principles shared by many healthy native populations. In his book *Native Nutrition: Eating According to Ancestral Wisdom* (Rochester, Vermont, Healing Arts Press, 1994), naturopath Ronald F Schmid examines the studies of native populations by Dr Weston Price and Dr Francis M Pottenger: the eskimos of Alaska, the Swiss of the Loetschental Valley, native Americans, Africans and South Sea islanders. All these populations, who lived on fresh fruits and vegetables, grains, wild game and fish, or healthy, free-roaming animals and, in some cases, fresh, unprocessed dairy products, were or are impressive for their strong, healthy bodies, perfectly straight teeth and freedom from the degenerative diseases currently plaguing us in the West.

Although their diets varied enormously (the African Maasai mainly eat meat, milk and blood, while the traditional Maori of New Zealand eat fish, kelp and roots), they share certain basic similarities. According to American dietary expert Annemarie Colbin in her book *Food and Healing* (New York: Ballantine, 1986), all these native diets have in common food that is fresh (or preserved naturally, whether smoked, dried or pickled), grown locally and organically, in season, and cooked by traditional methods.

Whenever possible, eschew packaged and processed foods, and anything that has been added to, refined, enriched or in some way interfered with. This would include most processed baked goods, canned sauces, commercial peanut butter, sweets, "cheese" foods, crisps and corn chips.

The benefits of essential fatty acids

Many nutritionists now believe that the lack of EFAs in our diet is the cause of all our modern day maladies. This seemingly magical substance appears to do the opposite of what saturated animal fats do; they enlarge blood vessels and make the blood less sticky. Vitamin B6 is an important co-factor in helping the body to metabolise EFAs into prostaglandins.

It's also important to consume a diet high in the omega-3 EFAs, which are found in fatty deep-water fish, such as salmon and tuna, as well as in fish-oil extract capsules and oils like linseed and walnut.

Most of the oils that you see in the grocery store have been partially hydrogenated or, in the process of pressing, exposed to heat, which can destroy EFAs. Instead, cook with butter or a small amount of unrefined, cold-pressed unsaturated oil, like safflower, soy, olive or sunflower. Olive oil can actually reduce hypertension by dilating the coronary vessels. In general, most European oils are less refined than those produced in the US. In fact, the safest course is to cook with extra virgin olive oil, which is still made by traditional methods.

The dangers of trans fatty acids

Most processed and low-fat foods, which are deficient in EFAs, can cause an imbalance in our bodies when consumed, which lowers the "good" cholesterol and increases the "bad" cholesterol (JAMA, 1996; 275: 759). One of the most dangerous of these low-fat foods appears to be margarine, made from hydrogenated oils.

Hydrogenation began after 1912, allowing polyunsaturated fats to compete in the marketplace with butter and lard. During hydrogenation, oils are heated up to a high temperature and hydrogen is then sent through the oils. In the process, trans fatty acids (TFAs) are produced; these artificial unsaturated fatty acids have a different molecular structure to those found in the tissues of humans and other mammals. This production process creates "trans isomers" of fatty acids, which resemble the chemical configuration of saturated fat (Lancet, 1994; 343: 1268-71).

The amount of TFAs in processed foods can range from 5 to 75 per cent of the total fat; neither US nor British law requires manufacturers to state the amount of hydrogenated fat in a product, only whether or not it is present at all (Lancet, 1994; 343: 1268-71). TFAs can have a "disastrous" effect on your body's ability to use EFAs, says nutritional expert Dr Leo Galland, author of *Superimmunity for Kids* (New York, E P Dutton, 1998). They are even more detrimental when heated, turning into something akin to the polymers in plastic.

Hydrogenated fats can be found in fast foods, such as chips and doughnuts, and in the vegetable oils contained in shortenings and biscuits. They account for up to 10 per cent of the content of some margarines. Other manufacturers, like Van den Berghs, the makers of Flora, have now removed hydrogenation entirely.

George V Mann, a doctor from Nashville, Tennessee who has researched and written extensively on the subject, argues that lipoprotein receptors in cells are impaired by TFAs. Since this impairment prevents the body from processing cholesterol-bearing, low-density lipoproteins, the cells crank up their rate of synthesising cholesterol, eventually leading to high levels in the blood. We know from numerous studies that blood cholesterol is quickly elevated in people who are fed TFAs (J Lipid Res, 1992; 33: 399-410).

An eight-year study of 85,000 women by Harvard Medical School found that those women eating margarine had an increased risk of coronary heart disease. Partially hydrogenated vegetable oils have not only failed to provide the expected benefits as a substitute for highly saturated fats, but have "contributed to the occurrence of coronary heart disease", the Harvard researchers concluded (Lancet, 1993; 341: 581-5).

The more TFAs you eat (and are stored in body fat), the greater your risk of heart disease. One Welsh study showed a strong association between TFA content in body fat and death from heart disease (Br J Prev Soc Med, 1975; 29: 82-90).

Dr Mary Enig, formerly of the Department of Chemistry and Biochemistry at the University of Maryland, who analysed the TFA content of some 600 foods, reckons that Americans eat between 11 and 28 grams of TFAs a day—or one-fifth of their total intake of fat. To give you some idea of how this occurs, one large portion of chips cooked in partially hydrogenated oil contains 8 g of TFAs, as does 60 g of imitation cheese (Townsend Lett for Docs, 1995; 139/40: 68-70). The Harvard study reckons that TFAs could account for 6 per cent of all deaths from heart disease, or 30,000 deaths a year in the US alone. And, of course, heart disease rates are high in northern European countries, where consumption of TFAs is high, but low in the Mediterranean countries, where TFA intake is low (the main dietary fat is olive oil).

An epidemic of heart disease can be directly linked to the introduction of partially hydrogenated fats in food, with the first major outbreak recorded in 1920. Before the First World War, when cheese and butter were dietary staples, death from coronary thrombosis was rare. At least three studies have also shown that the incidence of heart disease went down during times when countries stopped consuming margarine and returned to butter (like during the Second World War). Nonetheless, researchers have stubbornly linked heart disease to animal fats, found in butter, giving margarine manufacturers the opportunity to promote their products as being better for your heart.

The Harvard findings are not conclusive, however. The National Heart, Lung and Blood Institute in the US said the link between TFAs and heart disease has not yet been proven, and is contrary to the findings of the National Cholesterol Education Program. This study, again from the US, reviewed the same data but reached the conclusion that "trans fatty acids do not raise blood cholesterol to the rate that saturated fat does" (Lancet,

1994; 343: 1268-71; The Times, 24 May 1994; 1 June 1994; International Herald Tribune, 19 May 1994).

The influential EURAMIC study, which covered eight European countries and Israel, also suggested there is no conclusive evidence to show that margarine is linked to heart problems. But it did warn of a potential connection in countries which consume large quantities of margarine.

The EURAMIC study based its findings on two groups of men—one with a serious heart condition and another without any history of heart problems. The researchers discovered that both groups had similar levels of TFAs in their tissues (Lancet, 1995; 345: 273-8).

There may be another issue here. In Dr George V Mann's studies of the African Maasai, the young men had consistently low cholesterol concentrations, even though their diets were high in saturated fats from milk and beef. Dr Mann concluded that the Maasai, who got about 4 to 7 g of TFAs a day from cow's milk, were below the threshold at which the body's ability to metabolise fat starts to be impaired. In the US, the average daily intake of TFAs is between 12 to 20 g.

The story may even be more complicated than this. Perhaps the Maasai are protected because they eat whole foods—albeit those containing saturated fats—and not the adulterated ones consumed by most people in the West.

As if to muddle the picture of margarine completely, in the spring of 1999, two new margarine-like products which claim to lower cholesterol levels with daily use became available for sale in the UK and US. These spreads, Benecol and Take Control, are made from plant derivatives which the manufacturers claim reduce cholesterol levels by inhibiting the absorption of cholesterol in the digestive tract. Benecol is made from plant stanol ester, a by-product of wood pulping, and Take Control uses sterol esters made from soya bean extract.

In May 1999, the FDA finally approved the sale of both products in America. The agency said they were satisfied with the manufacturer's claim that these products are safe and had no reported adverse effects. Several studies show a beneficial effect on cholesterol levels from the plant esters in both spreads (N Eng J Med, 1995; 333: 1308-12; Eur J Clin Nutr, 1998; 52: 334-43; Am J Clin Nutr, 1999; 69: 403-10).

Indeed, these benefits seem impressive at first glance. Benecol claims to reduce total cholesterol by up to 10 per cent and LDL cholesterol by 14 per cent in people who eat three servings per day. Similarly, Take Control has been shown to lower total cholesterol by an average of 7 to 10 per cent when taken daily.

Although the cholesterol-lowering effect is impressive, it's no more so than an individual could achieve eating real food and taking regular exercise. Furthermore, dietary modification and exercise produce long-term effects, while the effect of plant esters only lasts as long as you continue to take them. In one study, two weeks after stopping treatment with stanol ester (sistostanol), cholesterol levels returned to pre-treatment levels (Atherosclerosis, 1986; 61: 219-23). This begs the question of whether these products are simply another attempt to find a magic bullet for heart disease.

Both spreads have been on the market in Finland since 1995, but this is a a very short time to assess long-term adverse effects. There is already some concern over the pseudo-hormonal effects of these new substances. Indeed, not long before the FDA's approval of the products, a Swedish review in 1998 made the disturbing observation that "further studies are required of [their] phyto-oestrogenic and endocrine effects, and [their] effects on growing children, particularly regarding subsequent fertility in boys" (Lakartidningen, 1998; 95: 5146-8).

This has not stopped the manufacturers of Benecol from planning an entire range of pre-packaged foods which feature their product and are aimed, according to a Benecol spokesman, at "cholesterol concerned" individuals everywhere.

Perhaps the most disturbing aspect of such spreads is that they sit on an uncomfortable fence between food and medicine. Surely this particular kind of plastic food is not what Hippocrates had in mind when he said, "Let food be your medicine and medicine your food."

The controversy over eggs

"Say no to the egg," wrote Dr Dean Ornish, assistant clinical professor of medicine at the School for Medicine, University of California at San Francisco, recently (New York Times, 15 Sept 1997). This American heart disease guru has done extensive research into reversing symptoms of heart disease without drugs or surgery. His regime—a combination of a low-fat (less than 10 per cent of calories as fat) vegetarian diet, plus exercise and stress reduction—has been shown to work when followed closely (Postgrad Med, 1993; 94: 50-65).

Part of his recommended diet is to limit or completely cut out eggs, which he says increase the risk of heart attacks. However, others, such as researcher Joseph Hattersley, disagree with Dr Ornish's criticism of eggs.

Hattersley argues that half the fat in eggs is monounsaturated—like olive oil—which resists oxidation and counters any cholesterol-raising effect (Curr Opin Lipidology, 1990; 1: 18-22). Even for the less than one per cent of people who are "hypercholesterolemic", eggs increase cholesterol little, if at all (Am J Clin Nutri, 1992; 55: 400-10; Arterioscl Thrombosis, 1994; 14: 576-86).

Cooked properly and eaten whole as nature made them, eggs are relatively low in the essential amino acid methionine. Excess methionine in red meat, milk and milk products is metabolised by healthy people into homocysteine (HC), which has been shown to be pro-oxidant, promoting hardening of the arteries, thrombosis, osteoporosis and even cancer (Ann Clinic Lab Sci, 1994; 24: 27-59).

Eggs are only dangerous when they are processed. Hundreds of processed foods containing powdered egg yolks are highly atherogenic: they damage arterial walls. Molecules of oxygen and cholesterol combine when heated in spray drying, creating "oxysterols" (Am J Clin Nutri, 1979; 32: 40-57) and only then making the cholesterol dangerous (Biochem Biophys Acts, 1987; 917: 337-40). Hot-scrambling of eggs exposes their cholesterol to oxygen with heat, creating abundant oxysterols.

Eggs are rich in EFAs and contain all eight essential amino acids (building blocks of high-quality protein) in the closest thing to perfect ratios. High quality EFAs, notably the omega-3s found in eggs, are scarce in processed Western diets and even in the official diets recommended by the American and British heart associations (Am J Clin Nutr, 1994; 60: 973-4). Organic eggs also provide a wealth of the minerals that are even lacking in organic vegetables and fruits.

The sulphur in eggs and the cysteine it generates are not only excellent in detoxification, but also good antioxidants (SA Rogers, *Wellness Against All Odds*, Syracuse, NY: Prestige Publ, 1994). Eggs contain eight times more of the cholesterol-lowering emulsifier lecithin than cholesterol does. Lecithin helps to keep the body's cholesterol fluid, preventing it from clogging up arteries (Lancet, 1992; 342: 810-3).

Another study has also recently helped to rescue the humble egg from the list of "bad" foods. Researchers at Harvard School of Public Health have found that eating one egg a day did not increase the risk of stroke or heart disease (JAMA, 1999; 281: 1387-94).

The Mediterranean approach

Many of the elements of what are now regarded as a healthy diet—meat used as a condiment rather than the centrepiece of meals, large helpings of fruits, vegetables, olive oil and fish—are present in the Mediterranean diet, the regime followed by many Southern European countries. Stacks of research now prove that this type of diet can help prevent heart attacks and even death.

One of the most astounding examples of this occurred in a prevention trial, comparing an adaptation of the Mediterranean diet, as followed in Crete, with the "prudent" diet usually prescribed to cardiac patients. After more than two years, all cardiovascular events, new heart attacks and deaths were decreased by 70 per cent among the group given the Mediterranean diet (Am J Clin Nutrit, 1995; 61: 1360S-67S).

This diet, followed by heart patients who were taking no other intervention, yielded results more than twice as good as the very best results achieved by cholesterol-lowering drugs.

When researchers of this Lyon Diet Heart Study attempted to find out why, they discovered that the protective effects had nothing to do with blood cholesterol levels (neither the good nor the bad type). Instead, they noticed differences in levels of essential fatty acids.

With the diet, there were higher intakes of linolenic and oleic acids (omega-3 fatty acids, from fish or flaxseed oils) and lower intakes of saturated fatty acids and linoleic acid (omega-6 fatty acids, from corn, safflower and soy oils). This increase in omega-3 fatty acids and oleic acid, plus the decrease in linoleic acid, proved protective.

A rich intake of antioxidants may also account for the protective effect of the diet. Higher levels of vitamins C and E were also recorded in patients on the Mediterranean diet. This finding seems consistent with other studies which have shown that high levels of vitamin E and beta-carotene lowered the risk of heart attack.

Common knowledge has it that Japan and the Mediterranean countries suffer far fewer heart problems than do people in the US and the north European countries. Mortality rates in Japan and the Mediterranean countries range between 4 and 5 per cent, compared to 12 per cent in the US and 15 per cent in northern Europe.

The one and only variation between these countries seems to be diet. Vitamins A and beta-carotene are also higher in the Mediterranean diet, and flavonoid intake is twice as high in Japan and the Mediterranean countries as in the US and northern Europe.

Quit smoking

Giving up smoking, which appears to exacerbate abnormalities of blood vessels in people with high blood cholesterol, is possibly one of the most meaningful lifestyle changes you can make (Circulation, 1996; 93: 1346-53).

CHAPTER 11

SPECIAL AIDS TO A HEALTHY HEART

As with research into the Mediterranean Diet, a University of Edinburgh study found that people with angina have significantly lower levels of vitamins C, E and the carotenoids (precursors of vitamin A) than do healthy individuals, and would likely benefit from supplements of these nutrients, particularly vitamin E (Lancet, 1991; 337: 1-5).

Studies of nearly 133,000 people, presented at the American Heart Association's annual meeting, also suggest that vitamin E can protect against heart disease. Women taking vitamin E for two years halved their risk, while men taking it for the same period of time had a 26 per cent lower risk.

Taking just a small amount of vitamin E (even just 25 IU daily) prevents LDL (the "bad" cholesterol) oxidation as well as the formation of blood clots. Two excellent studies from Harvard University demonstrate that those who take at least 100 IU per day of vitamin E reduce their risk of heart disease substantially. These studies concluded that 100 to 750 IU daily of vitamin E significantly reduces the incidence of angina and heart attacks (New Eng J Med, 1993; 328: 1444-9).

Vitamin E can even protect against alcoholic cardiomyopathy, commonly known as drinker's heart. But high doses of vitamin E are not recommended for those who suffer from hypertension, rheumatic heart disease and certain other conditions, except under the close supervision of a qualified health practitioner.

Older people who eat an orange a day during the winter have been found to reduce their risks of a heart attack by 10 per cent. Based on a one-year report on 96 men and women, aged between 65 and 74 years, researchers discovered that an extra 60 mg of vitamin C a day (the amount contained in one orange) could lower levels of the clotting agent fibrinogen in the blood, and so reduce the risk of heart disease (BMJ, 1995; 310: 1563-6).

This research from Addenbrooke's Hospital in Cambridge may help explain why more older people die in the winter than in the summer. Not only do risk factors for heart disease tend to increase in the winter months, but also people's average stores of vitamin C tend to fall as diets change during the colder seasons. During the summer, the average daily intake of vitamin C among the study group was 90 mg, which fell to 65 mg in the winter, possibly because there was a smaller selection of fruits and vegetables available.

Although many earlier studies had shown a link between heart disease and the various antioxidants, the Cambridge study is one of the first to scientifically measure the levels of vitamin C in the blood.

Other vitamins and minerals play an important protective role. Of these, magnesium shows the greatest promise. Deficiency in magnesium has long been thought to cause hypertension (J Exp Med, 1957; 106: 767-76; Am J Clin Nutri, 1959; 7: 13-22; Lancet, 1980; ii: 720-2). Recent studies have shown that the average daily intake of magnesium in men who later experienced heart disease is around 12 per cent lower than in patients without heart troubles (Br Heart J, 1988; 59: 201-6).

Intravenous infusion of magnesium salts, if given soon after a heart attack, has been shown to work as well thrombolysis or antiplatelet therapy (Lancet, 1992; 339: 1553-8), but with no long-lasting side effects.

Some practitioners argue that magnesium is less effective than standard treatments, usually quoting the ISIS-4 trial. However, in this leg of the large clinical trial investigating stroke and heart attack treatments, 7.64 per cent of patients receiving magnesium died, compared to 7.24 per cent in the standard treatment group (Lancet, 1995; 345: 669-85), demonstrating that magnesium is at least as effective as orthodox treatments.

L-carnitine

The amino acid L-carnitine could have an important role to play in helping people recover from various heart conditions, including acute heart attack. Carnitine is a naturally-occurring amino acid found in all living tissue, and its task is to transport long-chain fatty acids within cells. If you are low in this nutrient, these fatty acids can accumulate instead of being burned up to create energy. Any deficiency of L-carnitine could also deprive the heart of adequate oxygen.

The most impressive finding showed that supplements of the nutrient could help the heart expand to take more blood after an acute heart attack. Usually, after such an attack, portions of the heart muscle die, thus making it impossible to expand (J Cardiology, 1995; 26: 380-7).

In another trial, L-carnitine was tested alongside two heart drugs, propafenone and mexiletine, on 50 patients suffering from an irregular heartbeat. Some of the patients were given the supplement on its own, while others were given it in association with one of the drugs. After 14 days of treatment, the patients experienced a significant reduction of irregular heartbeats. The supplements also helped the drugs to perform better (Clinica Tera- peutica 1995; 146: 769-74).

In a third study, researchers found that L-carnitine could help heart-disease patients to exercise longer. The supplement helped to

131

increase the levels of the acid found in the blood supply after exercise which, in turn, improved walking capacity (Circulation, 1996; 93: 1685-9).

CoQ10

Co-enzyme Q10 (CoQ10), also known as ubiquinone, is a naturally occurring substance with characteristics in common with vitamins. It plays a vital role in the conversion of nutrients into energy and has become one of the most popular "new" dietary supplements of the last decade. Because it is so fundamental to the process of creating energy, almost every cell in the human body contains CoQ10. However, its concentration varies in different organs, with the highest in those which produce large amounts of energy, such as the heart, liver, kidney and pancreas (J Am Chem Soc, 1959; 81: 4007-10).

As well as boosting energy, it plays a role in preventing a wide range of diseases. With no known toxicity, it has been shown to normalise blood pressure, increase exercise tolerance and boost immunity, and it acts as an antioxidant.

Patients with cardiovascular diseases, such as angina, hypertension, mitrial valve prolapse and congestive heart failure, all require an increased tissue level of CoQ10 (Proc Natl Acad Sci, 1985; 82: 901-4; Drugs Exptl Clin Res, 1984; 10: 487-502).

The first review of CoQ10 concluded that this supplement offered a therapeutic benefit in approximately 75 per cent of cases of congestive heart failure. It also showed an improvement in patients with essential hypertension and angina (J Mol Med, 1977; 2: 431-60).

In a more recent study, 12 patients with stable angina were treated with CoQ10 (150 mg daily for four weeks) in a double-blind trial (Am J Cardiol, 1985; 56: 247). Compared to the placebo group, CoQ10 reduced the frequency of angina attacks by 53 per cent, as well as significantly improving exercise tolerance.

Heart-tissue biopsies in patients with various heart diseases have shown a CoQ10 deficiency in 50 to 75 per cent of cases (Int J Vit Nutri Res, 1972; 42: 413). This finding has been repeated in other studies of plasma levels of CoQ10 (Am J Cardiol, 1990; 65: 521-3).

It is believed that supplementing with CoQ10 may help prevent irregular heartbeat (J Exp Med, 1983; 141: 453-63), as well as cellular damage to the heart during a heart attack (J Clin Pharmacol, 1990; 30: 596-608). Although not all studies have been positive (Z Kardiol, 1989; 78: 360-5; J Neurol Sci, 1990; 100: 70-8), the overwhelming trend is that heart patients improve when supplemented with CoQ10.

There is no Recommended Daily Allowance for CoQ10, but the therapeutic daily intake is considered to be between 10 to 90 mg. It is probably most effective in an oil base, such as soya oil, since this aids absorption.

The best natural sources of CoQ10 are sardines and mackerel, pork, spinach, soya oil, peanuts, sesame seeds and walnuts. It can be synthesised in the body but is easily destroyed by the overuse of stimulants and sugar. Absorption is aided by the presence of B vitamins and iron.

Vitamin B6

Moses Suzman, the respected neurologist from South Africa, speculated long ago that a pandemic deficiency of B6 was the prime cause of heart attacks. Following his suspicions, from 1950 onwards he advised all of his patients to take two 50 mg tablets of B6 a day with meals. Apart from adding a daily B-complex after 1972, he urged no other change in their diet, supplements or lifestyle. They weren't even discouraged from smoking.

After 45 years, his thousands of current and former patients had far fewer heart problems than would be expected.

Dr Suzman prescribed 200 mg of B6 every day to his patients

who had a heart attack or chest pains, as well as folic acid, magnesium, vitamins E and C, selenium and other nutrients. After just a few weeks, these patients were successfully weaned off their heart medicines and, eventually, their arterial clogging reversed. Dr Suzman knew of no coronary artery spasm, cardiac arrest or stroke among all of his patients—even those with high blood pressure and stressful lives.

In 1962, a doctor called John Marion Ellis began using B6 to treat patients with carpal tunnel syndrome. Even though they were eating a typical Western processed diet, few of these patients went on to suffer a heart attack or had to undergo bypass surgery (Ann NY Acad Sci, 1990; 85: 302-20). Those who did were found to have symptoms of advanced vitamin B6 deficiency—diabetes, oedema and tingling in the fingers and hands.

Although many of Dr Ellis's patients took other supplements, improved their diets, exercised or quit smoking, those who took 50 to 200 mg of vitamin B6 every day over the decades had 73 per cent fewer chest pains and heart attacks than the others.

Vitamin B6 is believed to help convert the toxic, sulphur-containing amino acid homocysteine (HC)—a byproduct of the metabolism of methionine—into useful, generally non-toxic cystathionine. This byproduct is then converted into cysteine, which is critically important in normal brain function and in the detoxification of the hundreds of chemicals that you're exposed to every day.

In 1969, research pathologist Kilmer S McCully proposed that even slight elevations of HC—which promote the tiny clots that initiate arterial damage as well as the catastrophic ones that precipitate most heart attacks and strokes—puts one at risk of a heart attack (Lancet, 13 June 1981). In adequate amounts, vitamin B6 can prevent these clots which are responsible for starting arterial damage, shielding the heart from further damage.

If McCully is right, his discovery has stunning ramifications for the treatment of heart disease. The entire edifice of heart disease treatment—the millions spent on drugs and the latest in gee-whizz surgical techniques—could all be demolished in a stroke—replaced by a simple, inexpensive vitamin.

Fruits and vegetables

Researchers studied a group of nearly 11,000 health-conscious people, including both vegetarians and those who frequently ate wholemeal bread, bran cereals, nuts or dried fruits, fresh fruit and raw salad, and compared their mortality levels with the rest of the population. After tracking them for nearly 17 years, scientists from the Imperial Cancer Research Fund found that all the groups were half as likely to suffer from heart disease or stroke as the rest of the population. But among these healthy eaters, those who ate fresh fruit every day had a 24 per cent reduction in fatal heart disease, a 32 per cent reduction in death from stroke, and an overall 21 per cent lower mortality rate.

It was also discovered that vegetarians had a 15 per cent lower rate of fatal heart disease, while those who ate wholemeal bread every day had a 12 per cent lower death rate than the national average, and those who had a raw salad every day had a 26 per cent lower rate of fatal heart disease (BMJ, 1996; 313: 775-9).

A balance of the different essential nutrients is essential for maintaining health. While fruits and vegetables are commonly thought to be high in essential vitamins and minerals, the majority of today's fruits, vegetables and grains are grown in depleted soil and stored for long periods of time before being sold. They may be stored for an even longer time after purchase before actually being eaten or used in cooking.

One interesting study, which documented the historical decline in the mineral content of fruits and vegetables between 1930 and 1987, came up with some starling conclusions (Br Food J, 1997; 99: 207-11).

Modern potatoes, for instance, were shown to have 40 per cent less potassium in them than the old ones. Carrots contain nearly half the calcium they once did, and 75 per cent less magnesium. Among the fruits, apples contain two-thirds less iron than they once did, as do oranges and apricots. Tomatoes contain 90 per cent less copper. In general, across 20 common fruits and vegetables, the trend was that foods were less nutritious than they once had been.

These figures do not alter the fact that fruit and vegetables are vital sources of nutrients—perhaps the most important source. But for health-conscious individuals, especially vegetarians, a switch to organic foods—be they fruits and vegetables or meats—may be the best way to ensure optimum nutrient intake.

Soybeans
Soybeans can be an effective treatment for kidney patients whose cholesterol abnormalities increase the risk of heart disease. In patients with kidney disease, consuming a vegetarian soy diet for eight weeks resulted in significant falls in blood cholesterol and in urinary protein excretion. As soon as they reverted to a normal diet, blood cholesterol and urine protein levels returned to what they had been before.

According to the study, conducted by the University of Milan, the "soy diet induced a moderate but significant reduction in urinary protein excretion that. . . could not be attributed to spontaneous improvement".

Green Tea
Researchers from the Saitama Cancer Centre Research Institute in Japan studied the tea-drinking habits of 1,371 men in Yoshimi, Japan (BMJ, 1995; 310: 693-6). Frequent green tea drinkers were found to have lower cholesterol levels, and those who drank more than 10 cups a day were also protected against liver complaints. The same benefits were not found in regular drinkers of black tea, the more popular variety in the West.

Alcohol

Have you ever wondered why the French are so carefree about tobacco smoking and wine consumption? Their diet is high in sugars and fats, and vegetarianism is virtually unknown to them— a perfect recipe for strokes, heart attacks and atherosclerosis. However, paradoxically, the French have the lowest cardiovascular disease mortality rate in the western world (B Schwitters, J Masqueller, *OPC: In Practice, The Hidden Story of Proanthocyadine*; Rome: 1994).

This puzzling situation has been connected with red wine consumption, which in France rates among the highest in the Western world. But the life expectancy of French men and women is also among the highest in the world. It is the oligomeric proanthocyanidine (OPC) in the grape seeds processed in French red wine that has been found to have this amazing protective effect against cardiovascular degenerative problems (C Kilham, *OPC: The Miracle Antioxidant*, Keats Publishing, 1997).

The latest vindication of wine drinking was made by researchers from the Danish Epidemiology Science Centre in Copenhagen, which studied the drinking habits of 6,051 men and 7,234 women between 30 and 70 (BMJ, 1995; 310: 1165-9). They discovered that the risk of a heart attack falls in relation to the amount of wine consumed; those who drank more than six glasses of wine a day had the lowest risk of heart attack, whereas abstainers were at highest risk. Moderate wine drinkers—those who drank between three and five glasses a day—halved their chances of suffering a fatal heart attack or stroke.

As for other alcoholic beverages, the risk of having a fatal heart attack increased among spirit drinkers who drank the same quantities every day—spirits were beneficial only if drunk once a month. Beer seemed to have no effect either way.

These findings seem to reflect some of the health and social changes in Denmark, where fatal heart disease has fallen by 30 per cent in the past 15 years, while wine-drinking has nearly doubled. Researchers suspect that the ethanol in the wine may be responsible for the beneficial effect, as might the tannin in the red wine. Red wine also contains antioxidants and flavonoids, which are thought to protect against heart disease and some cancers.

But before we all raise a celebratory glass, the researchers were careful to point out that alcohol is also linked with cirrhosis, some cancers and violent death. Furthermore, the study didn't examine the other possibly detrimental effects of lost essential minerals, like magnesium, caused by wine, which is a natural diuretic.

Drinking alcohol may, however, be less beneficial if you are a woman. Scientists from the Channing Laboratory in Boston, Massachusetts, studied the health of 85,709 women for 12 years and discovered that while women also enjoy the protection against heart disease if they drink small amounts of alcohol, drinking may increase the risks of developing breast cancer. Those most likely to benefit from drinking alcohol were the women already at a high risk of suffering heart disease. Any benefits were lost if they drank more than 30 g of alcohol a day (a bottle of beer contains 12 g of alcohol), at which point deaths from breast cancer and cirrhosis increased dramatically (New Eng J Med, 1995; 332: 1733-7).

Fish

Scientists have been puzzling over the effects of eating fish on the heart ever since researchers noticed a low incidence of heart problems among the people of Japan and Greenland, both of whom have a diet rich in fish. Early research indicates that a fish diet could protect against a heart attack, and the omega-3 fatty acids in fish are thought to be responsible for these beneficial effects.

Analysis of existing data, carried out by the University College London Medical School, also concluded that fish oil is likely to help heart sufferers. It seems a fish diet can have particularly enormous benefits for those who have either already suffered a heart attack or had angioplasty, or for those with high blood pressure.

Another study has shown that even men with no heart disease, but with risk factors for heart disease, can benefit from adding fish daily to their diet. Researchers from Northwestern University Medical School in Chicago recruited 1,822 men aged between 40 and 55. Although these men were free of cardiovascular disease, on average they were all overweight and had too-high levels of blood pressure and cholesterol. Half were smokers and most were drinkers. Despite this, those who ate 35 g or more of fish enjoyed a far lower risk of heart disease (New Eng J Med, 1997; 336: 1046-53).

However, a more recent major study, which examined 44,895 men aged between 40 and 75 with no history of heart disease, suggests that this may not be the case. Researchers from Harvard found that the group which had fish just once a month suffered no more heart attacks than those who had fish six times a week (New Eng J Med, 1995; 332: 977-82).

Since then, a study of the eating habits of Tanzanian villagers has revealed that fresh fish raises the levels of n-3 polyunsaturated fatty acids in the blood and lowers both blood pressure and plasma lipid concentrations (Lancet, 1996; 348: 784-8).

Garlic

Some simple foods have amazing properties on the heart. There is much scientific evidence to back up garlic's reputation as a potent cholesterol-reducer of the blood. In one of the best studies, a number of German centres banded together to put garlic to the test under extreme conditions. They chose two months during Christmas and New Year to see whether the reputed benefits of garlic would stretch over the season with the highest cholesterol-laden meals.

Of the 43 patients studied in the randomised, double-blind, placebo-controlled trial, some were given a product containing garlic and *Ginkgo biloba* (Allium Plus) and the others, a placebo. After two months, 35 per cent of the treated group recorded improvement in cholesterol levels, which was significantly better than the average 10.4 per cent reduction in cholesterol found in the control group.

After the study, those treated abstained from taking Allium for two weeks. When their cholesterol levels were measured, they were found to be identical to the levels they started with, demonstrating that the garlic-ginkgo combination was definitely responsible for the lowering of cholesterol in the trial (Arzneimittel-Forschung, 1993; 43: 978-81).

Outside of the holiday season, standardised garlic powder tablets (such as Kwai and Sapec) have been shown to lower total cholesterol levels by an average of 12 per cent, and triglycerides by an average of 17 per cent (Arzneimittel-Forschung, 1990; 40: 1111-6).

Garlic has also been used to treat arterial disease of the legs. In one study, a daily dose of 800 mg of garlic powder enabled patients with intermittent claudication (cramplike pain on walking, due to arterial disease of the legs) to walk further than a matched set of controls. Interestingly, this increase in walking distance didn't occur until the fifth week of treatment—at the same time that the researchers observed a thinning of the blood. Blood pressure, cholesterol concentration and blood viscosity also decreased (Clinical Investigator, 1993; 71: 383-6).

CHAPTER 12

AT-A-GLANCE TIPS FOR A HEALTHY HEART

The following is an easy-to-follow guide to the recommendations outlined in this book. *If you have had any history of heart problems, only follow this programme under the supervision of a qualified, experienced professional. Also consult a professional with knowledge of nutrition about the doses of supplements to take, since these vary, depending on your individual needs.*

For healthy people and all heart patients

- Follow the Mediterranean-style diet, which is rich in fruits and vegetables and olive oil, with meat as a condiment, rather than the centrepiece of meals.
- Eat fish liberally.
- Eat whole, unprocessed, organic foods grown locally and in season and cooked by traditional methods.
- Eat eggs any way but fried or hot scrambled.
- Avoid all hydrogenated margarine and other hydrogenated oils.
- Engage in regular aerobic exercise.
- Take foods and supplements high in omega-3 fatty acids, from fish or flaxseed oils, which prevent disease by lowering triglyceride and cholesterol levels, and increasing the HDL "good" cholesterol levels (Am J Cardiology, 1995; 76: 459-62).
- Take magnesium supplements, which have been shown to lower risk of heart disease.

- Drink red wine in moderation—in great moderation (less than 30 g per day—one bottle of beer is 12 g) if you are a woman.
- Take at least 50 mg of B6 per day, which will lower levels of homocysteine.
- Maintain good intake of the antioxidant vitamins—vitamins A, C and E, the carotenoids and selenium—which all help to prevent heart attacks.
- Engage in regular relaxation—TM, biofeedback and the like.
- Enjoy your life. Change your job or any other part of your life if you don't like it.
- Love and be loved.

Here are a few recommendations for specific conditions:

For angina:

- Take supplements of the amino acid L-carnitine, which has been proven effective.
- Keep levels of the A, C, E antioxidant vitamins high. Even amounts of vitamin E as small as 25 IUs per day will stop the formation of blood clots.
- Increase your intake of thiamine. Low levels of this B vitamin also increase your heart attack risk (Am J Med, 1995; 98: 485-90).
- Take CoQ10, which has been shown to reduce frequency of attacks and to prevent damage to the heart during attacks.

For hypertension:

- Keep your weight down. Losing weight, if you're overweight, will lower blood pressure naturally.
- Engage in regular aerobic exercise.
- Cut out additional salt from your diet and avoid salty foods.
- Limit your intake of refined sugar and saturated fats.
- Avoid caffeine. Only two cups of coffee a day can raise your blood pressure, particularly when you are under stress.
- Avoid the Pill and NSAIDs, which raise pressure.

- Check your levels of lead and cadmium, which can cause hypertension.
- Cook with cold-pressed olive oil and use only unrefined polyunsaturated oils in your diet.
- Limit alcohol to one drink a day.
- Eat potassium-rich foods like bananas or take a potassium supplement, which will help to dramatically lower blood pressure.
- Take magnesium, which may also help to lower blood pressure.
- Get enough calcium, in food or supplements. Low levels of calcium may bring on hypertension. Make sure your levels of vitamin D3 are adequate to ensure better uptake of calcium (Hypertension, 1994; 7: 363-7).
- CoQ10 supplements can bring down blood pressure.
- *Note: do not take high levels of vitmain E except under the close supervision of a qualified health practitioner.*

To prevent stroke:
- Eat at least five portions of fruit and vegetables.
- Consume moderate amounts of red wine or red grapes.
- Eat plenty of walnuts, soya and canola oil—all good sources of alpha-lineolic acid.
- Start exercising today and get your children exercising early in life.
- Keep antioxidant vitamins A, C and E levels high.

For ischaemia, particularly in the legs:
- Taking 800 mg of garlic powder daily helps to increase walking distance.
- Take supplements of magnesium. Patients with ischaemia are found to have lower levels of magnesium.

For high cholesterol
- Try garlic or garlic powder. Eat liberal quantities of garlic and onions, which also have proven cholesterol-lowering effects.
- Drink green tea, which has been found to lower cholesterol levels.

143

If you have already had a heart attack:

- Intravenous infusions of magnesium, given soon after a heart attack, have been shown to work as well as thrombolysis or antiplatelet therapy.
- Increase your levels of antioxidants, which can decrease the possibility of future heart attacks.
- High levels of vitamin B6 (take more than 100 mg per day only with medical supervision) may protect your heart from further damage.
- Take L-carnitine, which will help protect you from future attacks.
- Thiamine supplements after a heart attack help your heart's ventricular function improve (Am J Med, 1995; 98: 485-90).

With heart surgery:

- Vitamin E and high-dose vitamin C will protect your heart during bypass surgery, as will relaxation exercises after the surgery (J Thor Cardio Surg, 1994; 108: 302-10; Thor Cardio Surg, 1994; 42: 276-8).

CHAPTER 13

FURTHER READING

Julian M Whitaker, *Reversing Heart Disease* (New York: Warner Books, 1988).

Burton Goldberg, *Heart Disease* (Tiburon, CA: Future Medicine Publishing Inc, 1998).

Kilmer S McCully, *The Homocysteine Revolution* (Los Angeles: Keats Publishing, 1997).

Patrick Holford, *Say No To Heart Disease* (London: Piatkus, 1998).

Vernon Coleman, *High Blood Pressure* (Barnstaple, Devon: European Medical Journal, 1996).

Jillie Collings, *Beat Heart Disease Without Surgery* (London: Thorsons, 1995).

Dean Ornish, *Reversing Heart Disease* (London: Century, 1991).